The *Bali* Cookbook

The Bali Cookbook

Lonny Gerungan

photography by Warren Bright

KYLE CATHIE LTD

I dedicate this book to my parents, John Gerungan and Antoinette Roemahlaisalan, who gave me the opportunity to become who I am now.

I would also like to thank the following people for their help and assistance in the compilation of this book: Bpk Dewa Beratha, Governor of Bali; Ben Holthuis; IGN Wisnu Wardana (Bali Travel News Magazine); Drs I Ketut Wiana Mag (Master of Hindu religion); Mrs Lastri (Badung Tourism Department); Nyoman Asra; High Priest Ida Sri Mpu Rekadnyana Sidhanta; Jro Putu Artini; Gustra; I Gede Kusuma Dana; Priest Jero Mangku Sadri; Made Jana; Komang Sujana; I Gede Tarmada; Nyoman Pasek; Ibu Made Ariani; Anak Agung Bawa; Ida Bagus Nghurah Kumbayana; Raden Ayu Dewi Cahyaningrum; Made Wagiariyasih (Kadek); Ida Bagus Udiana; Ida Ayu Suci; I Wayan Rimpi; Meme Sari; Desa Seni (Canggu) and staff; Hotel Puri Santrian (Sanur) and staff; The International Media Services; Assistance & Communications Bali (Johan Hensen, Indra and Merti); Hanri Vaassen; Roy Gerungan and Wayne Gerungan.

First published in Great Britain in 2007 by Kyle Cathie Limited
122 Arlington Road, London NW1 7HP
general.enquiries@kyle-cathie.com   www.kylecathie.com

10 9 8 7 6 5 4 3 2 1

ISBN 978-1-85626-715-1

Editor:	**Hennie Franssen-Seebregts**
English editor:	**Danielle Di Michiel**
Art director:	**www.pinkstripedesign.com**
Photographer:	**Warren Bright** (except pages 76 and 91 from iStock, and page 109 from Corbis, Dave G. Houser/Corbis)
Copy editor:	**Sally Somers**
Proof reader:	**Vanessa Kendell**
Indexer:	**Alex Corrin**
Production:	**Sha Huxtable and Alice Holloway**

Lonny Gerungan is hereby identified as the author of this work in accordance with Section 77 of the Copyright, Designs and Patents Act 1988.

A Cataloguing in Publication record for this title is available from the British Library.

Colour reproduction by Colourscan
Printed in China by C & C Offset

For more information on Lonny, please visit www.lonnys.info

Contents

Foreword from the author   7

Foreword from the Governor of Bali   8

Before you start cooking   9

Bali: the last paradise on Earth   10

Meat   18

Poultry and eggs   56

Fish and seafood   84

Vegetables   114

Rice   144

Sambals   152

Sweet delicacies & drinks   164

Basic ingredients   184

Glossary of ingredients   186

Index   191

Foreword from the author

The Bali Cookbook is more than just a collection of recipes. This is a book that also paints a picture of the daily life of the Balinese, whose existence is centred on and guided by the Hindu faith. In everything they do and in every aspect of their lives, they will always take the gods into account. Visitors to Bali are made to feel extremely welcome and are invariably greeted with a warm smile. The gods have instructed the Balinese to be kind to every person they meet and to approach every undertaking in a positive manner. This open and engaging manner, so characteristic of the Balinese, not only endears and charms the tourists, but earns them a better existence in a subsequent life.

Honouring the gods and seeking favours from them, are an integral part of life. Throughout their lives, the Balinese make countless offerings to the gods and participate in numerous temple ceremonies. Such offerings will nearly always incorporate a food element and no temple ceremony would be complete without a huge festive meal – offered first to the gods and subsequently relished by all participants.

So it is hardly surprising that most of the dishes that the Balinese eat on a daily basis are related to their faith in one way or another and often form an intrinsic part of religious celebrations. Authentic Balinese cuisine is inseparably bound to the Hindu faith, which arrived on the island some 900 years ago, and had a profound influence on the culture.

During the writing of The Bali Cookbook I researched the rules, precepts and traditions of the many Balinese who still experience their religion in much the same way as their ancestors did. I discovered that religion is very much alive among my fellow Balinese and that matters of faith are treated with great reverence in the course of day-to-day living.

Over the centuries, some of the ideas behind certain precepts and traditions have been lost, but the traditions themselves remain. I find it remarkable, and sometimes amusing, that there is still such a strong adherence to tradition, but often only because it has been learned and passed on from parents and grandparents. When I asked about the preparation and consumption of certain dishes during temple ceremonies, I would often be told, with a shrug, that a particular dish was prepared 'because that's the way it is supposed to be'.

The Balinese are not used to recording their recipes on paper – for centuries the preparation has been handed down orally from one generation to another – and some authentic dishes have sadly been irretrievably lost. I wrote The Bali Cookbook not only as a way of disseminating the very special culture of my fellow islanders throughout the rest of the world, but also to prevent more of these recipes, with their added spiritual significance, being lost to future generations.

I hope you enjoy The Bali Cookbook, which was the result not only of hard work but of great love, devotion and pleasure on my part.

Lonny Gerungan.~

Foreword from the Governor of Bali

Om Swasttiastu (may God bless you)

On behalf of the Balinese people and the Bali Provincial Government, I would like to express our pride at the achievements of our Balinese son, Lonny Gerungan. Not only is he the expert on culinary Bali and Indonesia, but he makes the perfect 'goodwill ambassador' for Bali.

His many culinary books on Bali and Indonesia, DVDs, CDs and the TV programmes in Holland have made a great impression of Bali as well as allowed fans to try out our cuisine and share the exquisite taste of our island.

There is no doubt that these activities have led to the need for this new international book. We are honoured that through this book people from all over the world are now able to experience the unique taste of Balinese food.

I do hope that the authentic recipes, as well as Lonny's own created recipes, combined with the outstanding photography, will inspire readers to try out some of the mouth-watering delicacies that Lonny has selected for you. Hopefully it will inspire you to visit the tropical island of Bali. *The Bali Cookbook* will reveal the secrets of Balinese cooking, bringing you an extraordinary experience and delicious feast for the palate.

Selamat Menikmati
(Enjoy Balinese food)

OM SANTIH SANTIH SANTIH OM
(Peace to you)

Best regards

Dewa Beratha
Governor of Bali

before you start cooking

All information about Balinese ingredients listed in the recipes can be found in the ingredients glossary on pages 186–190.

Spice pastes

It is often said that a spice paste made in a food processor does not differ from one made with a *cobek* (mortar) and *ulekan* (pestle) but that is not true. I prefer the *cobek* because it produces a smooth paste with a very intense flavour. In a food processor, the herbs and spices are not really ground or crushed; they are smashed and the oils that are so important to the final flavour of the dish are not released. Often during the processing, a little water or oil needs to be added as well. The food processor can be used to break up the ingredients, after which they can be pounded to a pulp in the *cobek*.

Remove the stems from fresh long chillies and bird's eye chillies. If you do not like your food too hot, you can also remove the seeds and membranes of the chillies. Roll each chilli between the palms of your hands or on a hard surface so that the seeds are loosened from the membranes. Split the chilli open lengthways and you should be able to shake out the seeds easily. Finely slice the chillies.

Use whole spices rather than ground, as they will release a better, more aromatic flavour. Coriander and peppercorns, cumin seeds and cloves can be toasted briefly in a dry, hot frying pan until they start to release their aromas.

Using banana leaves as wraps

Buy fresh or frozen banana leaves. Cut off a piece that is large enough to hold the food, rinse it under running water and pat it dry.

Put a portion of the food or the ingredients listed in the recipe on the leaf, fold it over the filling and enclose it like an envelope. Secure the parcel with thin bamboo stalks or with toothpicks.

Steam the parcels on both sides over a charcoal fire, gas fire or steamer.

Rice

The recipes in this book are based on the Western custom of eating less rice than is common in Indonesia. The number of servings or portions indicated in each recipe is for a meal of rice and fish, meat or poultry, plus a vegetable dish. When you prepare a meal with various main and/or side dishes, reckon for an average meal for one person on approximately 75–100g of uncooked rice, 250–350g of meat, fish and poultry and 200–250g of vegetables, tofu and tempeh.

Bali *The last paradise on Earth*

Undoubtedly, Bali is the best known island of the Indonesian Republic, but it is certainly not the largest. Indonesia consists of nearly 14,000 islands, of which 6,000 are uninhabited. It is not a large island; from east to west, it barely measures 150 kilometres, and is just 80 kilometres from north to south. The international reputation of Bali is largely due to its impressive landscape, religion, culture and, above all, its friendly inhabitants. For centuries, Bali was a 'forgotten island', with a life all of its own. The inhabitants had scant or no contact with those of the other islands. As the island was not particularly rich in resources, the colonial powers left the Balinese to their own devices. The herbs and spices that Bali had to offer were of no interest to merchants, and valuable raw materials could not at that time be exploited. The 'discovery' of Bali by Westerners before the Second World War is mainly due to a small number of artists and art-lovers who happened upon the creativity of the Balinese; they discovered beautiful paintings and sculptures, all of which seemed to be created effortlessly. Then in the 1950s, the rich and famous found their way to Bali, lured by tales of a paradise inhabited by an artistic and hospitable people, paving the way for the hundreds of thousands of tourists who now visit the island each year.

Below: Typical Balinese rice terrace.

Bali is often called the 'last paradise on Earth', and it is easy to see why. The miniature island boasts a colourful vegetation, created partially by nature and partially by man. Thousands of terraced rice paddies cover the mountain and volcano slopes like a lush green blanket. The island houses almost 3.5 million inhabitants, and in order to provide daily sustenance to everyone, the Balinese have to use the available space very carefully. Out of sheer necessity, the people of Bali have taken over great tracts of nature to help provide their daily needs – by creating rice paddies. Yet this takeover seems to have happened harmoniously, as the paddies alternate with virgin tropical forests from which rivulets of the purest spring water flow downwards and eventually come together in mighty streams. And everywhere on Bali you can see stunning, colourful flowers.

And the Balinese? They treat the land and vegetation with the utmost respect and still live in harmony with nature, letting nature govern they way they live and not the other way around. Bali is referred to as the 'last paradise on Earth' not only because of its splendid vistas and white beaches with swaying palm trees, but also because the busy daily life of its inhabitants is still at one with creation and the natural beauty of the island.

Island of the gods

Above: Village temple.

Bali is also justly known as the 'island of the gods'. Almost 95 per cent of the Balinese people adhere to the Hindu dharma faith, a religion in which the original Hindu faith is combined in a unique way with elements from Buddhism and beliefs from animism. This faith enthrals the Balinese in each and every way and determines both the rhythm and practical arrangements of daily life. Everything a Balinese does is measured against his or her faith. The Balinese make offerings every day and not a week passes without ceremonies being performed exactly as distant ancestors performed them – young and old, dressed in colourful costumes, honour the gods, pacify the demons and thank and greet their deceased forebears. There is an estimated 30,000 temples of varying sizes, all devoted to the many and diverse gods that make up the Hindu pantheon. Wherever you go on this island, you will always find a temple, even in the smallest villages.

The ever-growing flood of tourists since the Second World War has inevitably brought profound changes. Some parts of the island have been all but completely taken over by tourism, with hotels and restaurants sprouting up to match demand.

Once idyllic paths through rice paddies are now
covered by asphalt, and, naturally, the impact of
the ever-increasing number of cars is evident in
many places. Temples which for centuries enjoyed
a serene calm have now become tourist hotspots.
But even in the face of mass tourism and
modernisation, the Balinese have managed to retain
the characteristic harmony of the island. Tourists have
become a welcome and highly profitable source of income
for Bali, and although it is sometimes said that the entire
island has turned into nothing but a tourist fair, this is plainly
nonsense. It is true that the tranquillity of some parts of the island has
been sacrificed in the interests of tourism, and that commercialism is at times blatant,
but for the most part Bali retains an air of having come to a standstill centuries ago. The
locals are well aware of the inherent 'dangers' of the annual mass influx of tourists, but
they are equally aware that the income generated from this raises their existence to a
higher level and ensures that the culture that surrounds them can be safeguarded for
the future. It should not be forgotten that the Balinese adore the interest the world
shows in their island, its culture, history and faith.

As a province of the Republic of Indonesia, Bali has its own government,
located in the capital, Denpasar. The island lies south of the equator and is
separated to the west from Java by the Bali Strait and to the east from Lombok
by the Lombok Strait. The Bali Sea lies to the island's north side, with the
Indian Ocean to the south.

Bali has a surface area of approximately 5,600 square kilometres with the
highest point at Gunung Agung (Mount Agung), an active volcano that rises
3,142 metres above sea level. On the slopes of this volcano is the best-known
and most important temple of Bali: the Pura Besakih. Each inhabitant of Bali
will visit this 'Mother Temple' at least once a year. They make offerings to the
gods in order to receive luck, health and prosperity in the upcoming year.

Ceremonies to guide the rhythm of life

Offerings to the gods determine both the daily rhythm on Bali and many other things besides. Details of when, where, how often and in what form the offerings should be were laid down centuries ago in holy writings on which the Hindu faith is based. Holy lontar books – stacks of artfully bound dried palm leaves on which the priests recorded, by hand in old Balinese script, the faith and its precepts – contain the prayers or mantras used to address the gods, magical formulae, ritual guidelines and directions on how to be a proper human, as well as the cycle of religious ceremonies and how they must be performed. These precepts are still strictly adhered to. Offerings form an integral part of the ceremonies governing all aspects of life for the Balinese, and signify a showing of respect for and gratitude towards everybody and everything in their environment. Of these, the gods and demons are the most important and must therefore never be forgotten. The Balinese make offerings to the gods out of pure gratitude for their existence and the gifts they have received on Earth in the forms of food, drink, friendship, affection and contentment. The demons receive offerings to keep them sweet, so to speak, and to prevent them from disturbing the daily rhythm of life in a negative manner. In this way, offerings to the demons are exclusively in order to keep mishaps and misfortune at bay. Offerings to the gods and demons represent two sides of the same coin, so that an offering to the gods automatically entails an offering to the demons. One cannot exist without its counterpart. Also important are offerings to the souls of the ancestors, and to the saints, of which the Hindu faith has a large number. In certain ceremonies, there are also offerings for the wellbeing of all fellow men, through which the Balinese demonstrate their unselfishness.

Above: A dancer performs the famous Legong Kraton. A traditional dance of femininity and grace, originally staged for royalty, now a favourite for tourists.

Bottom left: Temple offerings of fruit and cakes topped with coconut palm leaves.

The way an offering should be made is prescribed in great detail in the holy lontar books. It must be made from perishable materials, and the item offered can only be presented to the gods once during each offering. The simplest offerings are made from natural materials: palm and banana leaves, which are folded into boat or cup shapes and into which rice, meat or chicken and some flowers are placed. It is not only tradition, but also the duty of every Balinese family to make two such simple offerings each day to the gods, demons and ancestors. It happens in and near the house temple and in places with a special significance for the family, such as a water well, the *warung* (food stall), or another place that is vital to the income or wellbeing of the family. In the morning, offerings are made once the woman of the house has finished cooking. Family members may only eat after a small amount of every dish has been offered to the gods, ancestors and demons. According to the precepts the woman should be dressed in traditional Balinese costume and the offering sprinkled with some holy water. A burning incense stick is also present. With a graceful movement of her hand, she wafts the incense smoke upwards, the essence of the offerings rising with the smoke to the gods. The same ritual is repeated in the afternoon. Although the offering is chiefly a 'woman's job', it can also be performed by a man, in which case he too must wear traditional Balinese clothes. A number of rules have to be taken into account in any ceremony. The holy lontar books do not specify the size of the offerings, but the daily ones are usually simple. Each Balinese family is 'required' to make offerings in accordance with its status. For poor people a small, simple offering suffices, whereas more is expected from the well-to-do. Scrimping on offerings would invite calamity for the Balinese individual in question as well as for his or her family.

Temple offerings

When the occasion is a temple ceremony, both rich and poor put more time, money and effort into their offerings. Depending on the importance of the ceremony, which is recorded in the holy lontar books, preparations start well ahead of the actual event.

When a ceremony for the family temple is to take place, the women in the family divide the tasks, which consist mainly of making decorations for the temple, and offerings. The men are in charge of preparing the ritual food. Although men are allowed to make decorations and offerings, women are not allowed to participate in the 'kitchen activities' which precede a ceremony. On such days, the men need to get up very early, because the cattle to be used for the meat offering must be killed before sunrise. Next, they clean and prepare the herbs and spices that will go into the various dishes served later. All this takes place in the *banjar*, a communal space found in every Balinese village. By then the women have usually finished preparing the offerings, which consist mainly of different fruits, rice cakes, one or more small dishes and some flowers.

Below: Small offerings are made every day.

The offerings are arranged into colourful sculptures such as towers or pyramids. These are placed on a beautiful platter which is carried on the head to the temple. When the ceremony takes place in the village temple, the women will often form a parade and walk to the temple in a colourful procession.

Once at the temple, the towers are placed on a large podium. There they are all blessed simultaneously by the priest. After the ceremony, the towers are taken home again, where the fruits, cakes and various dishes are handed out to family members. Food that is ritually prepared by the men is always eaten in the temple after the conclusion of the ceremony. Many ceremonies specify and prescribe the type of ritual offerings that should be brought, and this determines which array of dishes will be eaten, and which will not, once the ceremony is over.

If it is a water buffalo being slaughtered, dishes using buffalo meat will be eaten, and the same applies to duck, chicken, turtle (the meat of this protected species can only be offered and eaten in a ceremony), fish, and so on. *Be guling*, spit-roasted suckling pig stuffed with typical Balinese herbs and spices, is included in every ceremony, but does not first have to be offered to the gods. For special temple festivals, the Balinese go to great lengths as far as food and drink are concerned. They prepare an enormous variety of dishes in order to show their willingness to do everything in their power to please the gods, and the communal meal forms a vital part of the tradition of a temple festival.

Above: Decorations for the temple offerings are made out of young coconut palm leaves.

Spicy Balinese cuisine

For centuries, the Balinese led a very isolated existence. Inhabitants of other parts of this archipelago were not interested in this island paradise, because it had little or nothing to offer in terms of making money. For hundreds of years, Bali was left alone by the rest of the world. This is why the Balinese can now boast a cuisine that is uniquely their own, a culinary tradition exposed to hardly any external influences for much of its history, and one which has therefore lost almost none of its authenticity. Balinese cooking retains a truly original character, one that rests on ingredients indigenous to the island, such as vegetables, fruits, herbs and spices.

It is no surprise that many people think of Balinese food as frugal. Although the island's volcanic soil, combined with a warm and moist climate conducive to growth, has always yielded a plentiful harvest, the harvest itself is not particularly diverse. Added to this is the fact that meat has always been very expensive – in part due to the isolated existence of the island – and so not often eaten, and that fish cannot be served every day, on religious grounds. And so it becomes clear that the cuisine consists mainly of 'green' dishes. However, it cannot be said that Balinese food is monotonous, thanks to the creative and, at times, intricately complex use of herbs and spices, which go towards creating extraordinary taste sensations.

Although still largely authentic, Balinese culinary tradition has seen some changes over the years. It is an age-old adage that, as far as meat is concerned, the Balinese will eat anything that walks, crawls and swims. They can wax lyrical about the taste of dragonflies, crickets, ants and bee larvae, as well as hedgehogs, lizards, sawa eels and sea turtles. These kinds of meat were eaten almost daily in the past and the true Balinese still enjoy eating them, although less frequently these days. However, you will not find many of these items on the menu of a Balinese restaurant.

Changes in the cuisine

The influx of tourism, which has given the island a major economical boost since the second half of last century, has brought with it a change in eating patterns. Pork, beef and poultry dishes, in the past only eaten on feast days, have become more common. The practice of eating fish has also seen some changes. The Balinese have never been fond of fish, partly because they believe that the waters surrounding the island are populated by demons and evil spirits. They instinctively shy away from any evil that may confront them and this in turn influences the cuisine in terms of fish consumption. That many Balinese now make fishing their livelihood, and that the markets display a wide variety of fresh fish can be attributed to the influence of tourism, as can the increased sales of various types of vegetables that are not traditionally found growing on the island. These have been introduced by foreigners and have become extremely sought after by chefs working in international hotels and restaurants.

Bali's prolonged isolation over the centuries has given rise to a very particular branch of Hindu faith. The Hinduism that the Balinese adhere to originated in India, and although there are many similarities between the faith on Bali and that in India, there are some notable differences as well, some evident in the cuisine. In India, for example, the faithful do not eat beef, whilst those on Bali do (with the exception of those belonging to the so-called Brahmans, the highest caste from which the priests are recruited).

The daily meal

When there is no feast or ceremony, the Balinese simply eat when they are hungry – there are no fixed mealtimes. It is still customary for the woman of the house to prepare all the food for the day in the morning. First of all, she goes to the market or to the *warung*, a small stall by the wayside, to buy everything she needs, before returning home to prepare the food. Rice and vegetables are the staples of the daily meal, and usually a modest piece of meat or fish is added. When the food is ready, a small part of it is offered to the gods and the ancestors in one of the shrines of the house temple. Only then can the Balinese partake of the food themselves. The dishes are placed on a table in the kitchen and the food is left for everyone to help themselves whenever they want. This means that fish, meat and vegetable dishes are not usually eaten warm, and only the rice, kept covered all day, must be warm before serving.

The Balinese do not consider everyday eating to be a communal affair. As a rule, they eat three times a day – in the morning, afternoon and towards evening – but only when they are hungry and have time to eat. After helping themselves to some food, they find a secluded spot or sheltered corner where they can enjoy a quiet meal.

Typical Balinese flavours

The main difference between Balinese cuisine and other Indonesian cuisines is in the use of two basic spice pastes, *base megenep* (also called *base genep*) and *base wangenan*. Prepared by pounding different herbs and spices on a flat mortar and mixing them together afterwards, both were originally intended to mask and neutralise the strong flavours of pork, duck and goat meat. Gradually, they became an integral part of Balinese cooking . The most typical ingredients are shallots, ginger, long pepper, garlic, candlenuts, lesser galangal, bird's eye chillies, dried shrimp paste, lime, turmeric, galangal, palm sugar, tamarind, coriander, nutmeg, benzoin, cinnamon, cloves and salt.

Almost every dish is eaten with the condiment *sambal*: a very sharp paste-like sauce based on bird's eye chilli peppers (*rawit*) and long, fresh chilli peppers (*lombok*). Bali boasts its own *sambal* sauces: *sambal matah* and *sambal mbe*. These are prepared daily at home and are served super-fresh in most restaurants. Another item particular to Balinese cuisine is the flavour of *kecap manis*, a sweet and syrupy soy sauce to which palm sugar has been added.

Opposite page: A farmer collects a papaya.

This page: Lonny roasts a chicken while preparing be siap mepanggang *(see page 64).*

The kitchen gods

The average Balinese is not very particular about the kitchen, which is usually situated under a lean-to outside the house and in which a wood fire is the main source of heat. There are still many Balinese men and women who, before cooking, will make obeisances to Om Brasina, the god of fire. The offering will generally consist of a few colourful flowers and some grains of rice strewn around the fire. Failure to make this offering could result in the god of fire becoming disgruntled and causing the dishes to burn, or otherwise fail.

A somewhat lesser part in Balinese life is played by Malipa and Malipi, the god and goddess of the kitchen. Most people are not even aware of the existence of these gods, and not much is known about their background and origin. When I started work on this book, I was told there should still be some very old clay statues of this kitchen god and goddess in the Bali National Museum in Denpasar. They were indeed listed on the inventory of the museum, but no one was able to find them. Officials surmised that the statues had been stolen, but a notice in the local media provided the answer: Malipa and Malipi had some years previously been given to someone as a gift and were still in the recipient's house in perfect condition. The statues, probably the only ones of their type in existence, are now back and on display in the museum.

Meat

Meat is considered a delicacy on Bali, but the Western habit of serving meat as the most prominent feature of a dish is not the Balinese way. Meat remains expensive and scarce, which is why it is only served as a side dish to the daily meal. Only at religious festivals do the Balinese eat copious portions of meat, during a communal meal after the ceremony in the temple, as well as at weddings or after a cremation. Rice is the daily main dish, and to give it extra flavour the Balinese add *sambal*, vegetables, deep-fried shallots, egg, fish, prawn crackers and a little bit of meat.

The Balinese love pork, and in this regard they are at odds with the majority of their countrymen; as Islam is the dominant faith in Indonesia, pork is considered unclean and not fit for consumption. The Hindu faith, however, does allow pork to be eaten, and the Balinese consume it with great enthusiasm. All over Bali you can see the characteristic dark pigs which often have an enormous belly. The meat from these pigs forms the basis of the best-known Balinese dish, *be guling* – eaten with every ceremony and whenever there is something to celebrate. *Be guling*, or *babi guling* as the Indonesians call it, is prepared from a three- to six-month-old pig weighing between four and six kilos. After the animal is killed, the hairs are removed and the skin rubbed with turmeric, which will lend it a beautiful golden colour during the spit-roasting. It is then stuffed with herbs and spices, and the belly is sewn up. The pig is roasted for several hours on a spit over a fire made from coconut shells and husks, and to prevent burning, the spit is turned continuously. It is this action (*guling* means turning) that gives this dish its name.

Once the meat is cooked, the rind – which becomes wonderfully crisp from the roasting – is removed and the meat cut into portions and served. The Balinese love the crisp rind and they are also fond of the spicy filling, which is served in small portions alongside the meat.

Pork has always been and still is much cheaper than beef, which helps to explain why pork is so ubiquitous in Balinese cooking. Beef comes mainly from the light brown Balinese cow (with its characteristic white behind). These cattle can be seen grazing around the rice paddies on the island, or ruminating under shelters constructed specially to protect them from the burning sun. Many dishes containing either pork or beef are braised in *santen*, or coconut milk, because the meat is on the tough side and needs long braising in order to become edible and digestible. Minced meat, on the other hand, can be steamed – wrapped in banana leaves in the same way as so many fish dishes. Like elsewhere in Indonesia, goat meat features on the menu. Among the most well-known goat dishes is *sate kambing*, a satay of goat meat that is cut into small pieces and threaded onto sticks. These are freshly roasted on street stalls all over the island, and are served with a sauce of sweet and spicy *kecap* with ground peanuts and finely chopped shallots.

Kambing mekuah

goat in spicy coconut sauce

Priests, always of the Brahman caste (which is the highest caste on Bali), are especially fond of this dish. Once ordained, priests are obliged to lead a simple and sober life, foregoing many delights, some of which are culinary in nature. They are not allowed to eat beef, pork or chicken dishes, which leaves just goat on the menu. Priests, unlike 'ordinary' people, are not allowed to enjoy foods being offered to the gods. 'Ordinary' visitors to the temples love eating the food offerings because of the extraordinary powers the foods are believed to contain.

serves 4–6

750g goat meat, cubed
3 lemongrass stalks
16 tablespoons vegetable oil
9 cardamom pods
150g *Base Megenep* (page 185)
1½ tablespoons white
  wine vinegar
300ml boiling water
salt
600ml thin coconut milk
  (page 184)
7 shallots, peeled and
  thinly sliced
leaves from 3 sprigs of Asian
  celery, finely chopped

Bring a large pan of water to the boil. Add the goat meat, reduce the heat and simmer for about 10 minutes. Drain and discard the cooking liquid.

Trim the lemongrass, bruise the stalks and tie the leaves together in a knot.

Heat 4 tablespoons of the oil in a wok and fry the lemongrass, cardamom pods and *base megenep* until light brown. Add the meat, vinegar and water. Season with salt and simmer until the water is almost evaporated.

Add the coconut milk and bring slowly to the boil on a low heat. Simmer for about 45 minutes until the meat is tender.

Meanwhile, heat the remaining oil in a wok. Deep-fry the shallots until crisp and golden. Using a slotted spoon, transfer them to kitchen paper and leave to drain.

Garnish the meat with the shallots and celery leaves, and serve with *Nasi Kuning* (page 148).

Be sampi base Bali

beef with Balinese spices

Indonesian and Balinese cuisine would not be complete without chillies, although they are not in fact indigenous to Indonesia. Some 500 years ago, the Spanish and Portuguese brought chillies from the New World and exchanged them for peppercorns. They used the relatively inexpensive chillies they discovered in South America to barter for Indonesian peppercorns, which in Europe were hugely expensive. Once the Indonesians discovered the flavour of chilli they were hooked, and the use of peppercorns declined. Through time, the chilli has become a key ingredient in Balinese cooking.

serves 4–6

750g stewing beef
1 lemongrass stalk
3cm piece of fresh galangal, peeled
3 tablespoons vegetable oil
3 kaffir lime leaves
3 salam leaves
1 tablespoon melted *gula Bali* or palm sugar
500ml warm water
500ml thick coconut milk (page 184)
salt

For the spice paste
7 candlenuts
7 shallots, peeled and finely sliced
3 garlic cloves, peeled and finely chopped
3 long red chillies, deseeded and sliced
5 bird's eye chillies, sliced
4cm piece of fresh ginger, peeled and finely chopped
4cm piece of fresh turmeric, peeled and finely chopped

To make the spice paste, use a pestle and mortar to pound the candlenuts to a fine paste. Add the shallots, garlic, chillies, ginger and turmeric and pound again to a paste.

Cut the meat into small pieces. Trim the lemongrass, bruise the stalk and tie the leaves together in a knot. Bruise the galangal.

Heat the oil in a wok and fry the spice paste for about 3 minutes. Stir in the pieces of meat, lemongrass, galangal, lime leaves, salam leaves and *gula Bali* or palm sugar. Stir-fry for about 5 minutes. Add the warm water, reduce the heat to low and simmer for about 45 minutes.

Add the coconut milk and bring to the boil. Reduce the heat and simmer for about 45 minutes until the meat is tender. Season with salt and serve with white rice and *Sambal Megoreng* (page 158).

Abon sampi

cooked and pounded beef

A simple but very tasty dish, particularly delicious with the neutral taste of *Nasi Putih* (white rice – page 147). I always sprinkle a little meat over the rice and eat it with *Sambal Mbe* (page 156). The herbs and spices make this a sensational dish.

serves 4–6

500g stewing beef, in one piece
5 salam leaves
300ml thick coconut milk
  (page 184)
12–15 tablespoons vegetable oil
5 shallots, peeled and thinly
  sliced
2 teaspoons coriander seeds
½ teaspoon white peppercorns
½ teaspoon black peppercorns
3 garlic cloves, peeled and finely
  chopped
5 long red chillies, deseeded and
  sliced
2 teaspoons *gula Bali* or palm
  sugar

In a large pan, bring 2.5 litres of water to the boil. Add the meat and the salam leaves and simmer for about 1½ hours. Remove the meat from the pan, discard the cooking liquid and salam leaves.

In the same pan, bring the coconut milk to the boil. Add the meat and simmer for approximately 30 minutes, until it has absorbed most of the milk. Remove from the heat and leave to cool.

Cut the meat into thin slices and, using a rolling pin, pound the slices of meat on a board until they are paper thin. Pull the meat apart into fine shreds.

Heat the oil in a wok. Deep-fry the shallots until crisp and golden. Using a slotted spoon, transfer them to kitchen paper and leave to drain. Fry the meat in the same oil until brown and crisp, then remove with a slotted spoon to kitchen paper to drain.

Using a pestle and mortar, pound the coriander seeds and peppercorns to a powder.

Pour all but 3 tablespoons of oil out of the wok. Add the garlic, chillies, ground coriander and pepper, and the *gula Bali* or palm sugar, and stir-fry for 2 minutes. Stir in the fried meat and shallots and serve as a side dish with *nasi campur* (white or yellow rice traditionally served on a plate with two meat or chicken dishes, vegetables and chilli sauce).

Be sampi base manis
beef in sweet kecap sauce

The Balinese believe in reincarnation. They are convinced they must do their utmost to please the gods if they are to come back into better circumstances in their next life. Showing respect for all living creatures is part of their life philosophy. So when an animal is slaughtered, an offering is made to ask for forgiveness. The Balinese are convinced that an animal slaughtered for food, so providing life sustenance, will in the next life be born onto a higher plane.

serves 4

750g stewing beef
6cm piece of fresh ginger, peeled
5 tablespoons vegetable oil
7 shallots, peeled and
    finely sliced
3 garlic cloves, peeled and
    finely chopped
5 tablespoons *kecap manis*
2 tablespoons *kecap asin*
1 teaspoon finely ground
    black pepper
500ml warm water
3 long green chillies, deseeded
    and sliced
3 long red chillies, deseeded
    and sliced

Cut the meat into 2cm pieces and bruise the ginger.

Heat the oil in a wok and fry the shallots and garlic for 2–3 minutes. Add the ginger and meat pieces and stir-fry for about 3 minutes.

Stir in the *kecap manis*, *kecap asin* and pepper and stir-fry for a further 1 minute. Pour the warm water over the meat and simmer for just over 1 hour, until tender.

Stir in the chillies and serve with *Nasi Kuning* and *Sambal Sere Tabia* (pages 148 and 159).

beef with coconut and beans

My advice is to use fresh herbs and spices whenever possible – the results will always be superior. Only in emergencies do I reach for dried or ground substitutes. Be especially careful when using ground ginger as, unlike other dried herbs and spices, it is considerably stronger than fresh ginger. The reason for this is because the active volatile oil, zingiberol, turns into shogoal during the drying process, and has twice the strength.

serves 2–3

200g stewing beef
100g fresh coconut
150g dried brown beans,
   soaked overnight
500ml water
50g sabah vegetable leaves
3 salam leaves
salt

For the spice paste
5 shallots, peeled and
   finely sliced
3 garlic cloves, peeled and
   finely chopped
7 bird's eye chillies, sliced
1 teaspoon roasted shrimp paste
3cm piece of fresh ginger,
   peeled and finely chopped
3cm piece of fresh galangal,
   peeled and finely chopped

Start by making the spice paste. Use a pestle and mortar to pound the shallots, garlic, chillies, shrimp paste, ginger and galangal to a paste.

Slice the beef into narrow strips. Remove the dark brown skin from the coconut and finely grate the flesh.

Put the presoaked beans and the meat into a pan, add the water and bring to the boil. Reduce the heat and simmer for about 1¼ hours until almost tender.

Add the sabah vegetable leaves, salam leaves, grated coconut and the spice paste. Season with salt and simmer for about 10 minutes until tender. Serve with *Nasi Kuning* (page 148).

Lawar sampi

spiced beef with coconut

There are only a few authentic beef dishes from Bali, which is of course related to the fact that beef is considerably more expensive than other kinds of meat. Another reason for the lack of enthusiasm for beef has to do with religion. In India, where the Balinese faith originated, the cow is sacred and the faithful there do not eat beef at all. On Bali, the rules do allow for eating beef, and some beef dishes, such as this one, act as offerings at religious ceremonies. These dishes are then thoroughly enjoyed, but in ordinary daily life the Balinese do not consume much beef. The beef rind gives this dish a kind of chewiness that no other ingredient can replicate.

serves 3–4

250g stewing beef, chuck or blade
125g beef rind
50g fresh coconut
50g fresh green peppercorns
75g *Base Gede* (page 185)

Put the beef in a large pan of boiling salted water. Reduce the heat and simmer for 2–2½ hours until tender. Remove the meat from the pan and chop it finely.

Meanwhile, simmer the beef rind for about 1 hour in another pan of boiling salted water. Drain and cut into small pieces.

Toast the coconut over hot charcoals or in a hot oven. Peel off the dark brown skin and coarsely grate the flesh. Chop half of the brown skin very finely and discard the remaining skin.

Mix the grated coconut with the chopped brown skin, peppercorns and *base gede*. Stir in the chopped meat and rind and serve with white rice.

stewed beef with jackfruit

The jackfruit used in this recipe is about three months old and therefore still unripe. If left to ripen on the tree, it can be picked about one month later. An unripe jackfruit, as is the case with other unripe fruits, is cooked and eaten as a vegetable. If you're worried that guests might not want to swallow a whole chilli, remove them before serving.

serves 3–4

500g stewing beef
500g young jackfruit
2 tablespoons vegetable oil
7 shallots, peeled and
    finely sliced
250ml thick coconut milk
    (page 184)
7 bird's eye chillies
salt

For the spice paste
1 teaspoon roasted shrimp paste
1 teaspoon black peppercorns
1 teaspoon sugar
2cm piece of fresh lesser
    galangal, peeled and
    finely chopped
3cm piece of fresh turmeric,
    peeled and finely chopped

Simmer the beef in boiling salted water for about 2 hours, until tender. In a separate pan, simmer the jackfruit in boiling salted water for about 15 minutes. Cut both the meat and the jackfruit into narrow strips.

For the spice paste, use a pestle and mortar to pound the shrimp paste, peppercorns and sugar to a fine paste. Add the lesser galangal and turmeric and pound again to a paste.

Heat the oil in a wok and fry the shallots until golden. Add the spice paste and fry for a further 3 minutes. Add the coconut milk, meat, jackfruit and chillies. Season with salt and simmer for a further 10 minutes. Serve with white rice and *Sambal Megoreng* (page 158).

Pindang sampi
spicy beef

Lemongrass is used in dishes not only for its refreshing lemony flavour, but also because it aids digestion.

serves 4

750g lean stewing beef
5 kaffir lime leaves, very
    finely sliced
750ml water
1 lemongrass stalk
150g *Base Gede* (page 185)
salt

Cut the beef into cubes. In a pan, bring the lime leaves and water to the boil, reduce the heat and simmer gently until the water turns green. Trim the lemongrass, bruise the stalk and tie the leaves together in a knot.

Add the *base gede*, lemongrass and meat to the water. Season with salt and simmer for about 1½ hours until the meat is tender. Serve with white rice and *Sambal Matah* (page 155).

Sate empol sampi

minced beef satay

For a long time it was difficult for tourists to enjoy authentic Balinese food on Bali. The Balinese dishes featured on menus were in fact Indonesian dishes. Even now the most authentic Balinese dishes are prepared for ceremonial occasions, which is the best time to get to know the cuisine. But in the last couple of years, I have noticed the emergence of small restaurants that serve traditional Balinese food. These are often run by locals who have discovered that many tourists greatly admire the island's specialities.

makes about 30/serves 6

12–15 tablespoons vegetable oil
7 shallots, peeled and
   finely sliced
500g minced beef
50ml thick coconut milk
   (page 184)
salt
3 tablespoons melted *gula Bali*
   or palm sugar

For the spice paste
3 garlic cloves, peeled
   and finely chopped
5 bird's eye chillies, sliced
3cm piece of fresh turmeric,
   peeled and finely chopped
juice of 2 leprous limes (if
   unavailable, use kaffir limes)

about 30 flat, wide satay sticks

To make the spice paste, use a pestle and mortar to pound the garlic, chillies, turmeric and lime juice to a paste.

Heat the oil in a wok. Deep-fry the shallots until golden and crisp. Using a slotted spoon, transfer them to kitchen paper and leave to drain.

Mix the minced beef with the spice paste, coconut milk, a little salt, the shallots and the melted *gula Bali* or palm sugar. Using your hands, shape heaped tablespoons of the mixture onto the satay sticks.

Grill the satays over a charcoal fire or under a hot grill for about 8 minutes, until brown and cooked through. Serve with white rice, *Sambal Megoreng* and *Jukut Urap* (pages 158 and 128).

Be sampi mesitsit

dry spicy beef

I always recommend using a flavourless oil for deep-frying and sautéing in these recipes, be it soy oil, rice oil, peanut (groundnut) oil or corn oil. These all have a fairly neutral taste, unlike olive oil, which is too strong and can overpower dishes and destroy the authentic Balinese flavours. Olive trees do not grow on Bali, and olive oil is not, and should not be, used in Balinese cooking. Coconut oil, until it developed a reputation for being unhealthy, was originally the oil of choice, but it has gradually fallen out of favour. However, research is now showing that coconut oil is healthy after all, which is good news as it lends exactly the right flavour to a dish.

serves 4

750g stewing beef, thickly sliced
2 tablespoons vegetable oil
1 tablespoon melted *gula Bali*
  or palm sugar
juice of 3 leprous limes
  (if unavailable, use kaffir limes)
salt

For the spice paste
2 teaspoons coriander seeds
1 teaspoon black peppercorns
2 teaspoons roasted shrimp paste
5 garlic cloves, peeled and
  finely chopped
3 long red chillies, deseeded
  and sliced
5 bird's eye chillies, sliced
4cm piece of fresh galangal,
  peeled and finely chopped

Bring a large pan of salted water to the boil. Add the meat and simmer for about 1½ hours until it is meltingly tender and can be shredded. With a fork, shred the meat into long, fine strips.

To make the spice paste, use a pestle and mortar to pound the coriander seeds, peppercorns and shrimp paste to a fine paste. Add the garlic, chillies and galangal and pound again.

Heat the oil in a wok and fry the spice paste for about 3 minutes. Add the meat, melted *gula Bali* or palm sugar and lime juice and stir-fry until the meat is quite dry. Serve with white rice and *Sambal Tomat* (page 159).

Serapah daging
beef with spicy sauce

Shallots feature in most Balinese dishes, both to enrich and to prevent sickness and stomach upsets. They are in fact a general cure-all.

makes about 30/serves 6

700g stewing beef, in one piece
12–15 tablespoons vegetable oil
5 shallots, peeled and
   thinly sliced
3 garlic cloves, peeled and
   thinly sliced
3 tablespoons rice flour
75ml water
3 tablespoons coconut oil
3 salam leaves
salt

For the spice paste
5 shallots, peeled and
   finely sliced
3 garlic cloves, peeled and
   finely chopped
5 bird's eye chillies, sliced
½ teaspoon roasted shrimp paste
3cm piece of fresh ginger, peeled
   and finely chopped
2cm piece of fresh lesser
   galangal, peeled and
   finely chopped
3cm piece of fresh turmeric,
   peeled and finely chopped

Bring a medium-sized pan of salted water to the boil, add the meat and reduce the heat. Simmer for about 2 hours until tender. Remove the meat from the pan (reserving the cooking liquid) and slice it thinly.

To make the spice paste, use a pestle and mortar to pound the shallots, garlic, chillies, shrimp paste, ginger, galangal and turmeric to a paste.

Heat the vegetable oil in a wok. Deep-fry the shallots and garlic separately until golden and crisp. Using a slotted spoon, transfer them to kitchen paper to drain.

Mix the rice flour with the water.

Heat the coconut oil in a wok and fry the spice paste and salam leaves for about 3 minutes. Add 300ml of the reserved cooking liquid and season with salt. Whisk in the flour mixture and gently simmer until the sauce has thickened.

Arrange the meat slices on a platter, pour the sauce over and sprinkle with the deep-fried shallots and garlic. Serve with white rice.

Balung kikil
spicy pig's trotters

This is a dish traditionally eaten by the poor on Bali and one that is in danger of disappearing. Pig's trotters are inexpensive, because they are considered to be a 'waste product', with more bone than meat. But they happen to be extremely good!

serves 6

12–15 tablespoons vegetable oil
7 shallots, peeled and
   thinly sliced
5 garlic cloves, peeled and
   thinly sliced
150g *Base Gede* (page 185)
2kg pig's trotters, chopped
   into pieces
5 salam leaves
2 litres boiling water
3 long red chillies, halved
   lengthways and deseeded
3 long green chillies, halved
   lengthways and deseeded

Heat the oil in a wok. Deep-fry the shallots and garlic separately until golden and crisp. Using a slotted spoon, transfer them to kitchen paper and leave to drain.

Pour all but 3 tablespoons of oil out of the wok and reheat the remaining oil. Add the *base gede* and stir-fry for about 3 minutes. Add the pig's trotters and salam leaves and stir-fry for a further 5 minutes. Add the water, reduce the heat and simmer for 1½–2 hours.

Stir the chillies along with the deep-fried shallots and garlic into the sauce and simmer for a further 5 minutes. Serve with white rice.

roasted suckling pig with Balinese spices

Whenever there is something to celebrate on Bali and people get together for a meal, *be guling* or *babi guling*, as it is also called, is sure to be served. The flavour of this dish is mainly due to the use of *base gede*, a truly distinctive taste in Balinese cooking. The stuffing is eaten as a vegetable, and the crackling, which everyone adores, is served as a delicious side dish.

Preparing *be guling* is somewhat time-consuming. The pig usually takes at least five hours to spit-roast and must be turned continuously. On Bali, dried coconut husks are used as fuel, and the aroma penetrates the meat, giving it extra flavour. I doubt very much if anyone has room in their kitchen for spit-roasting a suckling pig, but you can just spread the spice mixture over a piece of pork belly, roll it up, secure it with toothpicks and cook it in the oven at 200°C/400°F/Gas Mark 6. This is what I do at home for my guests.

serves 20–24

7cm piece of fresh turmeric
salt
1 oven-ready suckling pig,
    about 4–6kg
2 quantities *Begala* (page 116)
1.2kg *Base Gede* (page 185)
5 salam leaves
vegetable oil, for basting

Make a turmeric juice by grating the piece of fresh turmeric, mix it with 1 tablespoon of water, then press out the liquid in a tea sieve. You should have about 5 tablespoons of juice.

Rub salt over the pig and inside the cavity. Stuff the stomach cavity with the *begala*, *base gede* and salam leaves. Close the cavity and tie with kitchen string to secure. (On Bali, the stomach cavity is held together with sharp bamboo sticks, but satay sticks and toothpicks will work just as well.)

Rub 2 tablespoons of the turmeric juice over the skin so that it becomes yellow and glossy.

Run the spit through the pig and roast over coals (or coconut husks, as on Bali), turning continuously, for 3½–4 hours, until the meat is tender and the crackling crisp. Baste regularly with oil and remaning turmeric juice.

Remove the suckling pig from the spit and slice the crackling and the meat. Serve with white rice, *Urutan*, *Sambal Mbe* and *Jukut Ares* (pages 43, 156 and 120).

Be celeng base Bali

pork with Balinese spices

Candlenuts are used throughout Indonesia. It is often thought that these nuts are harvested just as you see and buy them in the shops. However, the nuts have a rock-hard dark brown shell that has to be removed first. On Bali, this is often done by a priest during a ceremony – thank goodness, as it is incredibly hard work! The nut itself is light yellow and has a fairly soft structure. Candlenut is so called because the nuts were once ground to a paste with copra and cotton to make candles. Shelled candlenuts are very perishable and must be stored in an airtight container. Buy in small quantities and only the amount you need.

serves 4

600g fillet of pork
4 tablespoons vegetable oil
5 kaffir lime leaves
1 teaspoon granulated sugar
salt
100ml hot water

For the spice paste
7 candlenuts
1 teaspoon coriander seeds
½ teaspoon white peppercorns
½ teaspoon black peppercorns
7 shallots, peeled and
    finely sliced
3 garlic cloves, peeled and
    finely chopped
8cm piece of fresh ginger,
    peeled and finely chopped
2cm piece of fresh lesser
    galangal, peeled and
    finely chopped
3cm piece of fresh turmeric,
    peeled and finely chopped

To make the spice paste, use a pestle and mortar to pound the candlenuts, coriander seeds and peppercorns to a fine paste. Add the shallots, garlic, ginger, lesser galangal and turmeric and pound again to a paste.

Thinly slice the pork and heat the oil in a wok. Add the spice paste and fry for about 3 minutes. Add the lime leaves and pork slices and stir-fry for a further 3 minutes. Add the sugar and season with salt. Add the water and cook for 5 minutes. Serve with *Nasi Kuning* and *Jukut Urap* (pages 148 and 128).

Be celeng gerangasem base Bali

braised marinated pork

For this recipe I use a braising pan because most people outside of Asia use this kind of pan for simmering meat. However, you can use a wok instead. There are different kinds of woks. Throughout Indonesia, a wok (*wajan*) with two handles is the pan of choice, though more and more people are buying the Chinese wok with one handle. The wok originally comes from China, but these days has a permanent place in virtually every kitchen.

serves 4

750g stewing pork
150g *Base Gede* (page 185)
1 lemongrass stalk
3 tablespoons vegetable oil
1 teaspoon roasted shrimp paste
3 salam leaves
3 kaffir lime leaves
1 litre boiling water

Cut the meat into small pieces, mix with the *base gede* and leave somewhere cool to marinate for 2 hours.

Trim the lemongrass, bruise the stalk and tie the leaves together in a knot.

Heat the oil in a wok and fry the shrimp paste, salam leaves, lime leaves and lemongrass. Add the marinated pork and the water. Simmer for about 20 minutes, then reduce the heat until the liquid is barely simmering and cook for about 30 minutes until tender. Serve with white rice.

Be celeng base manis
pork in sweet kecap sauce

For the locals, *Be Guling* (page 34) is certainly the most popular pork dish, but for tourists it has to be *be celeng base manis*, which on menus is usually called *babi kecap*. For those of you who have difficulty eating hot foods or simply do not care for them, this is the dish for you. I often serve this to my guests because it is delicious, quick and easy to make.

serves 4

3 tablespoons vegetable oil
7 shallots, peeled and finely sliced
3 garlic cloves, peeled
  and finely chopped
6cm piece of fresh ginger,
  peeled and finely sliced
600g pork shoulder or loin,
  cut into 2cm cubes
4 tablespoons *kecap manis*
2 tablespoons *kecap asin*
1 teaspoon finely ground
  black pepper
3 long red chillies, deseeded
  and sliced
3 long green chillies, deseeded
  and sliced
200ml boiling water

Heat the oil in a wok and fry the shallots and garlic until golden. Add the ginger and pork and stir-fry for about 2 minutes. Stir in the *kecap manis* and *kecap asin* and stir-fry for a further 1 minute.

Add the black pepper, chillies and water and braise the meat over a low heat for about 20 minutes until tender. Serve with *Nasi Kuning* and *Sambal Megoreng* (pages 148 and 158).

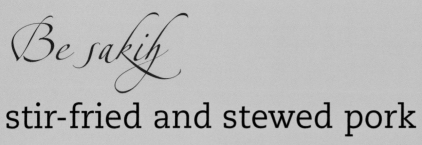

stir-fried and stewed pork

This recipe was given to me by Me Sari, owner of a *warung* (food stall) close to the Pura Besakih, the main temple on Bali. Ravenous after climbing endless stairs to the roof of the temple, I bought a snack at her stall. She was busy cooking and when I asked her what she was making, she told me that it was a recipe from her grandmother. She prepares it every day, but had long forgotten the name, so I have simply named it after the temple.

serves 4

600g boned shoulder of pork
5 tablespoons vegetable oil
3 salam leaves
salt
150ml stock or water

For the spice paste
5 shallots, peeled and
  finely sliced
3 garlic cloves, peeled and
  finely chopped
3 long red chillies, deseeded
  and sliced
11 bird's eye chillies, sliced
3cm piece of fresh ginger,
  peeled and finely chopped
3cm piece of fresh lesser
  galangal, peeled and
  finely chopped
5cm piece of fresh galangal,
  peeled and finely chopped
1 tablespoon tamarind pulp

Cut the meat in pieces of 3 x 1cm.

To make the spice paste, use a pestle and mortar to pound the shallots, garlic, chillies, ginger, lesser galangal, galangal and tamarind to a paste.

Heat the oil in a wok and fry the spice paste and salam leaves for about 3 minutes. Add the meat and stir-fry for about 5 minutes, then season with salt. Add the stock or water and simmer for about 20 minutes until the meat is tender and the liquid has reduced. Serve with white rice and *Sambal Tomat* (page 159).

Komoh celeng

spicy broth with pork

This dish is prepared for many ceremonies, but not offered to the gods. It is for the men who, early in the morning, begin cooking the dishes to be eaten after the ceremony during the *megibung* (collective meal for the men). Part of these dishes is offered during the ceremony, and they must not be eaten before this time.

serves 4–6

50g pork rind
1.25 litres water
150g pork shoulder
50g pork liver
2 tablespoons *Base Gede*
  (page 185)
12–15 tablespoons coconut oil
3 shallots, peeled and
  finely sliced
3 bird's eye chillies, sliced
1 teaspoon roasted shrimp paste
juice of 1 lime
salt

Put the pork rind and water in a large pan and bring to the boil. Reduce the heat slightly and simmer gently for about 1 hour. Remove the rind from the cooking liquid, set aside the liquid and cut the rind into small pieces.

Chop the meat and liver coarsely. In a bowl, mix the meat, liver and rind with the *base gede*.

Heat the coconut oil in a wok and deep-fry the shallots until golden brown. Using a slotted spoon, transfer them to kitchen paper and leave to drain.

Pour off all but 1 tablespoon of the oil and fry the chillies and shrimp paste for a few seconds. Stir the shallots, chillies and shrimp paste through the meat mixture and transfer to a deep serving dish.

Bring the reserved cooking liquid to the boil again and, stirring continuously, pour over the meat mixture. If you want to be sure the meat is cooked through properly, leave the boiling liquid to cook it for 5 minutes. Just before serving, squeeze the lime juice into the soup.

Lampiong

pork belly barbecued in banana leaves

serves 4

600g pork belly, with rind
5 shallots, peeled and finely sliced
3 garlic cloves, peeled and
    finely chopped
3 long red chillies, deseeded
    and sliced
9 bird's eye chillies, sliced
5cm piece of fresh ginger,
    peeled and finely chopped
3cm piece of fresh lesser galangal,
    peeled and finely chopped
2 teaspoons roasted shrimp paste
2 teaspoons *gula Bali* or palm sugar
1 large tomato, halved
salt

banana leaves
bamboo strips or toothpicks

Cut the meat into four long slices. Bring a large pan of water to the boil. Add the meat, bring back to the boil, then reduce the heat and simmer gently for 1–1½ hours until tender. Drain well.

Using a pestle and mortar, pound the shallots, garlic, chillies, ginger, lesser galangal, shrimp paste and *gula Bali* or palm sugar to a paste. Cut the tomato halves into slivers, then stir through the paste. Season with salt.

Cut out eight pieces of banana leaf, each large enough to hold a piece of meat. Place two pieces of leaf on top of each other and a piece of meat on top. Spread a quarter of the spice paste over the meat. Close to make a parcel and secure the sides with bamboo strips or toothpicks. Make three more parcels in the same way using the remaining ingredients.

Grill the *lampiong* for about 7 minutes on each side over hot coals or under a grill. Serve with white rice.

fried pork sausages

These sausages are always served with *Be Guling* (page 34). By using the spice paste *base gede*, they have a flavour that is typical of Balinese cuisine. You should be able to buy pig's blood from a good, traditional butcher.

makes 8–10/serves 4–5

500g pork shoulder or loin,
   coarsely chopped
3 salam leaves, very finely sliced
3 tablespoons *Base Gede*
   (page 185)
150ml pig's blood
1 teaspoon finely ground
   white pepper
salt
1 metre sausage casings
5 tablespoons coconut oil

Mix the chopped pork with the salam leaves, *base gede*, blood, pepper and a little salt. Put the mixture into a pastry bag fitted with a smooth nozzle or in a sausage stuffer.

Run cold water through the sausage casings and gently ease the whole length of casing onto the nozzle. Squeeze carefully to fill the casings with the sausage mix, twisting at 10cm intervals to create sausage shapes. Bind with kitchen string.

Place the sausages in a steamer, ensuring they rest above the water, cover and steam for about 30 minutes. Remove and pat them dry.

Heat the oil in a wok and fry the sausages on all sides until golden. Serve with *Be Guling* (page 34).

minced pork with spicy grated coconut and *sambal mbe*

Dishes with *lawar* in their name are associated with temple ceremonies. They always contain grated coconut, herbs and spices, to which meat or vegetables are sometimes added. Originally, *lawar* was prepared only with turtle meat, but nowadays it is also made with other kinds of meat, usually pork. There are different kinds of *lawar*, each one with its own colour and each one dedicated to a god or goddess. *Lawar celeng putih* (pork with grated coconut) is white and dedicated to the god Vishnu; *lawar celeng barak* (pork, coconut and pork blood) is red and is dedicated to the god Brahma. For both, chop the ingredients for the **base gede**, rather than pound them, as the mixture should be coarse, not a paste.

serves 4

125g pork rind
250g pork shoulder
50g fresh coconut
50g (coarse) *Base Gede* (page 185)
salt
150g *Sambal Mbe* (page 156)

For lawar celeng barak
1 tablespoon pig's blood

Cook the rind for about 1 hour in boiling, salted water, then drain and cut the rind into narrow strips.

Lightly simmer the pork shoulder for about 45 minutes in salted water. Remove and chop coarsely.

Roast the coconut above coals or in a hot oven, peel off the dark brown skin, reserving half, and finely grate the flesh. Chop the reserved dark brown skin very finely.

Combine all the ingredients and the *sambal*, adding the blood if you're making *Lawar Celeng Barak*. Serve with white rice, *Komoh Celeng* and *Urutan* (pages 41 and 43).

'There are different kinds of *lawar*, each one with its own colour and each one dedicated to a god or goddess.'

salad with young coconut and pork

Originally, this dish was eaten at temple festivals, but is rarely made these days. This is a great pity, because it is an amazing, flavourful dish. It uses the immature green coconut in which the shell still has to form properly. On your visit to Bali, it is worth trying to find this dish, and happily, you can still come across it at small market stalls in north-eastern Bali.

serves 4–6

200g immature (young) coconut
75g pork rind
100g pork shoulder
3 tablespoons coconut oil
2cm piece of fresh ginger, peeled and finely chopped
2cm piece of fresh lesser galangal, peeled and finely chopped
2cm piece of fresh turmeric, peeled and finely chopped
2cm piece of fresh galangal, peeled and finely chopped
3 candlenuts, pounded to a paste
1 salam leaf
75g *Sambal Mbe* (page 156)
1 kaffir lime leaf, very finely chopped
1 teaspoon *Base Wangenan* (page 185)
salt

Put the coconut in a pan, cover with water and bring to the boil. Reduce the heat and simmer for 10 minutes. Drain, cool and cut the coconut into long, thin strips. Squeeze out as much water as possible.

Cook the rind for about 1 hour in boiling salted water, until tender. Drain, cool and cut into long, thin strips. Cook the pork shoulder for about 45 minutes in simmering water. Drain and chop coarsely.

Heat the coconut oil in a wok, add the ginger, lesser galangal, turmeric, galangal, candlenuts and salam leaf and fry for 3 minutes. Stir in the strips of coconut, pork shoulder, rind, *sambal*, lime leaf, *base wangenan* and season with salt.

Serve with white rice.

Lawar nangka

salad with jackfruit and pork

On Bali, the tropical fruit *nangka*, also known as jackfruit, is sometimes confused with *nangka belanda* (literally Dutch *nangka*), a popular sweet and tangy tropical fruit known too as sirsak or soursop. Both are large, hanging fruits and both have knobbly skins. In fact, they are not related to one another; the jackfruit is quite a bit larger than the soursop and they taste totally different.

The Balinese eat a lot of undercooked meat, but if you prefer your meat cooked through, just follow my alternative instruction.

serves 4

1 jackfruit, about 600g, peeled
50g pork rind
100g fillet of pork
juice of 2 limes
1 teaspoon coriander seeds
½ teaspoon ground nutmeg
2 cloves
2cm piece of fresh lesser
  galangal, peeled and
  finely chopped
2cm piece of fresh turmeric,
  peeled and finely chopped
3cm piece of fresh galangal,
  peeled and finely chopped
200g freshly grated coconut
125g *Sambal Mbe* (page 156)
salt

Bring a large pan of salted water to the boil. Add the jackfruit, bring back to the boil, then reduce the heat and simmer for about 25 minutes until tender. Drain, cool and chop coarsely.

Meanwhile, cook the rind for about 1 hour in boiling salted water. Drain, leave to cool, then cut into narrow strips. Chop the pork coarsely and knead with the lime juice. The lime juice should cook the pork but, if you're concerned, cook the pork with the rind for 15–20 minutes.

Use a pestle and mortar to pound the coriander seeds, nutmeg and cloves to a powder. Add the lesser galangal, turmeric and galangal and pound to a paste.

Mix all the prepared ingredients with the coconut, *sambal* and a little salt. Serve with white rice.

Tambusan celeng
pork steamed in banana leaf

To prepare this dish the authentic way requires a lot of work. On Bali, the stuffed parcels are steamed and cooled, then put into a dish of uncooked rice so that – as unlikely as it sounds – they can absorb the flavour of the rice. The following day the parcels are roasted, not over coals but in the crumbled ashes. Grab the chance to try this dish cooked in the traditional manner, if you are lucky enough to be offered it. It is absolutely delicious!

makes 15/serves 4–5

600g pork shoulder
3 shallots, peeled and
    finely sliced
salt
3 candlenuts
150g Base Megenep (page 185)
3 tablespoons coconut oil
100ml water
15 salam leaves

rice
banana leaves, washed and
    patted dry
bamboo strips or toothpicks

Cut the meat into 15 slices, each about 3 x 4cm. Knead the meat with the shallots and a little salt until the mixture is soft and pliable.

Use a pestle and mortar to pound the candlenuts to a fine paste, then mix with the *base megenep*.

Add the prepared meat to the *base megenep* and mix with the oil and water.

Cut 15 pieces of banana leaf, each about 10 x 15cm. Place a slice of meat on each leaf. Top with a salam leaf. Fold both sides of the leaf over the filling. Fold the open ends over and secure the parcels with bamboo strips or toothpicks.

Place the parcels in a steamer, ensuring they sit above the gently simmering water. Cover and steam for 20 minutes, then remove from the steamer, pat them dry and leave to cool.

Sprinkle a layer of raw rice over a large platter and arrange the parcels on top. Cover with a thick layer of raw rice and leave to stand overnight.

The following day, remove the parcels from the rice and roast them in the ashes of a charcoal or wood fire. Serve with white rice.

steamed spicy minced pork in banana leaves

Banana leaves are quite tough, but become more pliable and easy to fold after they are briefly soaked in hot water or toasted quickly over an open flame. To prevent the filling being exposed through a tear during steaming or roasting, I always add an extra layer of banana or salam leaf. I certainly recommend this when making *tum celeng*, because the parcels are not only steamed, but also roasted. These steps, including the preparation of *base gede*, are illustrated on the following pages.

makes 10/serves 4–6

50g pork rind
2cm piece of fresh lesser
    galangal, peeled and
    finely chopped
50ml oil
250g minced pork
50g *Base Gede* (page 185)
150g *Sambal Mbe* (page 156)
10 salam leaves

banana leaves, washed and
    patted dry
bamboo strips or toothpicks

Cook the pork rind for about 1 hour in boiling water, then drain and leave to cool. Cut into very thin slices.

In a pestle and mortar, pound the lesser galangal to a fine paste.

Heat the oil in a pan and fry the *base gede* for 3 minutes.

Combine the minced pork with the lesser galangal, pork rind and *sambal mbe*. Divide the mixture into 10 portions.

Cut 10 squares of banana leaf, each about 20cm. Place one salam leaf on each square and top with a portion of mince. Fold both sides of the leaf over the filling. Fold the open ends over and secure the parcels with bamboo strips or toothpicks.

Place the parcels in a steamer, ensuring they rest above the water, and steam until tender, about 10 minutes. Serve with rice or on their own as a snack.

Tim nyat nyat

braised pork in shallot sauce

On Bali, ginger (*jahe*) is considered to be a cure-all, effective for every ailment. Whether you have a cold or the flu, it is thought that ginger tea can lead to a quick recovery, helping to reduce a fever and headache. Pregnant women drink a cup of ginger tea before eating, to combat morning sickness. The Balinese are also convinced that regularly eating dishes with ginger helps prevent heart problems.

makes 15/serves 4–5

3 tablespoons vegetable oil
600g pork shoulder or loin, cubed
300ml hot water
5 salam leaves
salt

For the spice paste
5 candlenuts
1 teaspoon roasted shrimp paste
1 teaspoon black peppercorns
9 shallots, peeled and
    finely sliced
3 garlic cloves, peeled and
    finely chopped
5cm piece of fresh ginger,
    peeled and finely chopped

To make the spice paste, use a pestle and mortar to pound the candlenuts, shrimp paste and peppercorns to a fine paste. Add the shallots, garlic and ginger and pound again to a paste.

Heat the oil in a wok and fry the spice paste for about 3 minutes. Add the meat to the spice paste and stir-fry until brown. Add the water and salam leaves and season with salt. Braise the meat for 20–30 minutes until tender. Serve with white rice.

'All over Bali, ginger is considered to be a cure-all, effective for every ailment.'

Sate empol celeng

minced pork satay

This dish is always eaten during *galungan*, the annual family festival on Bali when the streets are decked out with *penjors* – long, slender, pliable bamboo sticks decorated with woven palm leaves. There are countless ceremonies during *galungan*, not only in village temples, but also in private temples in the home. In the days leading up to the festivities, all temples are cleaned and repaired. Deceased family members are then invited to come and visit the temple, where they are honoured, and offerings made to them. It is customary for everyone to return to the family home for the celebrations before *galungan* begins.

makes about 30/serves 6

12–15 tablespoons vegetable oil
7 shallots, peeled and finely sliced
50ml thick coconut milk (page 184)
juice of 2 leprous limes (if unavailable, use kaffir limes)
3 tablespoons melted *gula Bali* or palm sugar
500g minced pork
salt

about 30 flat, wide satay sticks

For the spice paste
3 garlic cloves, peeled and finely chopped
5 bird's eye chillies, sliced
3cm piece of fresh turmeric, peeled and finely chopped

Heat the oil in a wok. Deep-fry the shallots until golden and crisp. Using a slotted spoon, transfer them to kitchen paper and leave to drain.

For the spice paste, use a pestle and mortar to pound the garlic, chillies and turmeric to a fine paste.

Mix the spice paste with the shallots, coconut milk, lime juice, melted *gula Bali* or palm sugar, minced pork and a little salt.

Using your hands, shape the mixture into about 30 small balls and thread each onto a satay stick. Grill for about 10 minutes over hot charcoals or under a hot grill until brown and cooked through. Serve with white rice, *Sambal Megoreng* and *Jukut Urap* (pages 158 and 128).

Sate celeng asem
pork satay with tamarind

Tamarind, or *asam*, is the brown, sweet and sour pulp that is strained after soaking the fibres and seeds of tamarind pods in water. The fruits of the tamarind tree, which grow mainly in northern Bali, resemble bean pods. The seeds can be roasted and eaten as a snack. The Balinese say that women in early stages of pregnancy develop a craving for dishes made with tamarind.

makes about 30/serves 6

500g pork shoulder

For the marinade
5 bird's eye chillies, sliced
5 garlic cloves, peeled
  and finely chopped
3cm piece of fresh ginger,
  peeled and chopped
2 tablespoons tamarind pulp
salt
3 tablespoons melted *gula Bali*
  or palm sugar

30 satay sticks

For the marinade, use a pestle and mortar to pound the chillies, garlic, ginger, tamarind and salt to a fine paste. Stir in the melted *gula Bali* or palm sugar.

Cut the meat into small pieces, mix with the spice paste and leave to marinate for 1 hour.

Thread 4–5 pieces of meat on each satay stick and grill for about 8 minutes over hot charcoal or under a hot grill, turning occasionally, until brown.

Serve with white rice, *Sambal Megoreng* and *Jukut Urap* (pages 158 and 128).

Poultry and eggs

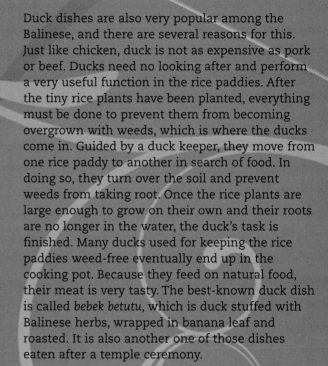

Chicken and duck dishes are great favourites on Bali. Both belong to the cheapest kinds of meat on the island, and many inhabitants can afford to have them on their menu regularly. You see chickens scratching about around houses all over Bali. They eat what nature has to offer, supplemented by mealtime leftovers, which makes them cheap to keep. The chickens that are busy around and between the houses are scrawny and do not deliver the same amount of meat as the farmed chickens that we know. However, chicken farms are springing up all over Bali, so plump, tender chickens are becoming available. Shops and restaurants offer both varieties, with the indigenous chicken, the so-called *ayam kampung* ('village chicken'), in great demand because of its natural flavour. These chickens are often seen in the high towers of fruit that women carry on their heads for offering to the gods at a ceremony in the temple.

As the priest blesses the towers, the essence of the food rises up to the gods. After the ceremony, the towers are taken home and the fruit and other foodstuffs eaten. The Balinese attribute special powers to this food and pieces of deep-fried chicken are stuck between or against the fruit. Before deep-frying, the chicken – always *ayam kampung* – is split open along the back and spatchcocked. After the ceremony, the chicken is eaten like this, but can often be turned into *be siap mesitsit* as well.

Duck dishes are also very popular among the Balinese, and there are several reasons for this. Just like chicken, duck is not as expensive as pork or beef. Ducks need no looking after and perform a very useful function in the rice paddies. After the tiny rice plants have been planted, everything must be done to prevent them from becoming overgrown with weeds, which is where the ducks come in. Guided by a duck keeper, they move from one rice paddy to another in search of food. In doing so, they turn over the soil and prevent weeds from taking root. Once the rice plants are large enough to grow on their own and their roots are no longer in the water, the duck's task is finished. Many ducks used for keeping the rice paddies weed-free eventually end up in the cooking pot. Because they feed on natural food, their meat is very tasty. The best-known duck dish is called *bebek betutu*, which is duck stuffed with Balinese herbs, wrapped in banana leaf and roasted. It is also another one of those dishes eaten after a temple ceremony.

There is one other reason the Balinese love duck so much: it is considered to be a very powerful animal, because it can survive both in water and on dry land. By eating the meat, a portion of this power is thought to be transferred to the eater! Of course, keeping chickens and ducks also means having a plentiful and ready supply of eggs, some of which are hatched out to maintain the stock. The rest of the eggs are used in the kitchen.

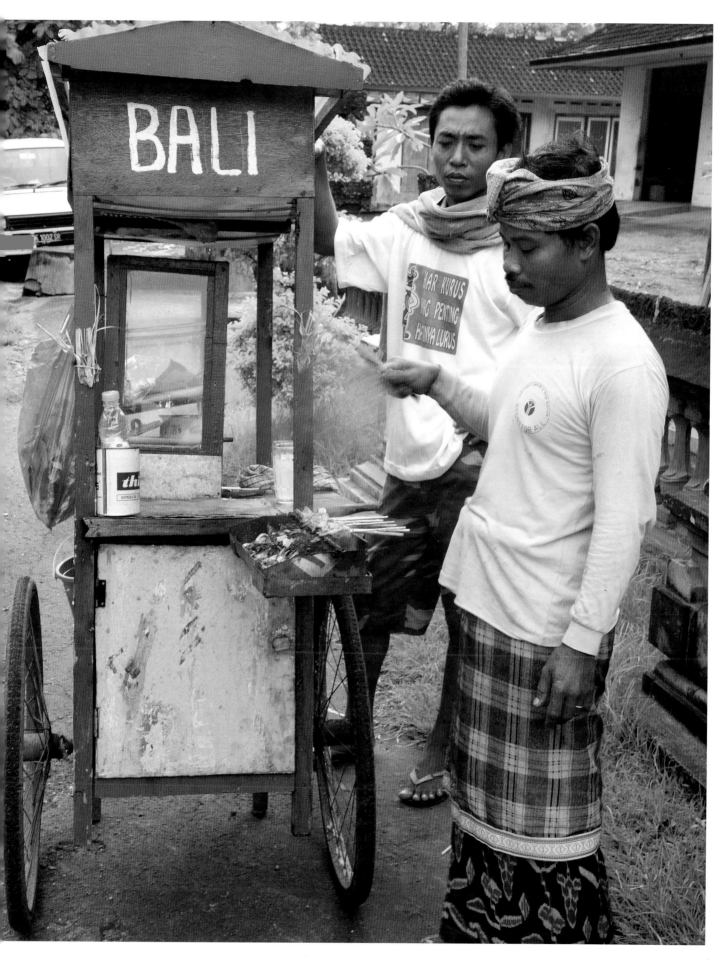

Be siap base Bali

chicken with Balinese spices

The leaf of the kaffir lime is used in many dishes for its fresh and lemony flavour. Used whole, they are not eaten but left to simmer in the dish and are removed just before serving. They can also be very finely sliced and mixed with the other herbs and spices used to make a spice paste, in which case they are absorbed in the dish and eaten.

serves 4

1 chicken, about 1.25kg
3 tablespoons vegetable oil
5 kaffir lime leaves
2 teaspoons granulated sugar
salt
500ml boiling water

For the spice paste
9 candlenuts
2 teaspoons coriander seeds
½ teaspoon white peppercorns
½ teaspoon black peppercorns
5 shallots, peeled and
   finely sliced
3 garlic cloves, peeled and
   finely chopped
3cm piece of fresh ginger,
   peeled and finely chopped
2cm piece of fresh lesser
   galangal, peeled and
   finely chopped
3cm piece of fresh turmeric,
   peeled and finely chopped

To make the spice paste, use a pestle and mortar to pound the candlenuts, coriander seeds and peppercorns to a fine paste. Add the shallots, garlic, ginger, lesser galangal and turmeric and pound again to a paste.

Cut the chicken into 4 pieces.

Heat the oil in a wok and fry the spice paste and lime leaves for about 3 minutes. Add the chicken pieces and fry briefly. Add the sugar and season with salt. Mix well and pour the water over. Simmer the chicken until tender, about 35 minutes.

Serve with *Nasi Putih* and *Sambal Megoreng* (pages 147 and 158).

Above: A Bali Aga village, the original people of Bali.

Be siap gerangasem

braised marinated chicken

Cock-fighting on Bali has long been a favourite pastime during which the *tuak* (palm beer) flows freely and betting is fierce. Nowadays on Bali, cock-fights are forbidden. Only when a cock fight is required for a certain temple ceremony do the police look the other way, and then the fight is allowed to go ahead in order to amuse the various demons. The blood of the defeated cock that flows over the ground is offered to the demons. The owner of the winning cock is allowed to take the dead opponent home for the pot. More often than not, a *siap gerangasem* is made with the bird.

serves 4

1 chicken, about 1.5kg
150g *Base Gede* (page 185)
5 tablespoons vegetable oil
1 lemongrass stalk
1 teaspoon roasted shrimp paste
3 salam leaves
3 kaffir lime leaves
1 litre boiling water

Cut the chicken into 12 pieces, mix with the *base gede* and about 3 tablespoons of the oil and leave to marinate somewhere cool for 2 hours. Trim the lemongrass, bruise the stalk and tie the leaves together in a knot.

Heat the remaining oil in a wide pan and fry the shrimp paste, salam leaves, lime leaves and lemongrass for 2 minutes. Add the chicken pieces and the water. Cook gently for about 20 minutes, reduce the heat to low and simmer for a further 1 hour.

Serve the chicken in the sauce with white rice.

Be siap base kalas

chicken in spicy coconut milk

Turmeric has a purifying effect and is often used in medicines prescribed for stomach complaints. For many Balinese, tea made from steeping grated fresh turmeric (about 20g), which is then mixed with the juice of half a lime, 1 teaspoon of honey and a pinch of salt, is a well-known home remedy for intestinal and stomach cramps.

serves 4

1 chicken, about 1.25kg
1 lemongrass stalk
3 tablespoons vegetable oil
3 salam leaves
400ml thick coconut milk
  (page 184)
1 tablespoon melted *gula Bali*
  or palm sugar
salt

For the spice paste
9 candlenuts
½ teaspoon white peppercorns
½ teaspoon black peppercorns
5 shallots, peeled and
  finely sliced
3 garlic cloves, peeled
  and finely chopped
5 bird's eye chillies, sliced
2cm piece of fresh lesser
  galangal, peeled and
  finely chopped
3cm piece of fresh turmeric,
  peeled and finely chopped
4cm piece of fresh galangal,
  peeled and finely chopped

To make the spice paste, use a pestle and mortar to pound the candlenuts and peppercorns to a fine paste. Add the shallots, garlic, chillies, lesser galangal, turmeric and galangal and pound again to a paste.

Cut the chicken into 4 pieces. Trim the lemongrass, bruise the stalk and tie the leaves together in a knot.

Heat the oil in a wok and fry the spice paste for about 3 minutes. Add the lemongrass, salam leaves and chicken pieces and stir-fry for about 2 minutes. Add the coconut milk, melted *gula Bali* or palm sugar and season with salt. Simmer the chicken until cooked, about 35 minutes.

Serve the chicken in the sauce with white rice.

Be siap mepanggang sambal sereh
grilled chicken with *sambal* sauce

serves 4

1 chicken, about 1.25kg
salt
2 teaspoons finely ground
  black pepper
juice of 3 leprous limes (if
  unavailable, use kaffir
  limes)
3 tablespoons vegetable oil
7 shallots, peeled and
  finely sliced
3 garlic cloves, peeled and
  finely chopped

5 long red chillies, deseeded
  and sliced
1 teaspoon roasted
  shrimp paste
3 lemongrass stalks, very
  finely chopped
5 kaffir lime leaves, very
  finely chopped

Table linen acquires a wonderful fresh scent
if you tuck some lemongrass stalks in it a
couple of days before you intend to use it.
Bruise the stalks and tie the leaves together
in a knot, as this helps to release their aroma.

Halve the chicken lengthways and rub both
halves with salt, black pepper and lime juice.
Grill the chicken for 50–55 minutes over a hot
charcoal fire or under a hot grill, until brown
and cooked through. Cut the chicken into
small pieces.

Heat the oil in a wok and fry the shallots,
garlic, chillies and shrimp paste for about
3 minutes. Add the lemongrass, lime leaves
and chicken pieces and stir-fry briefly. Serve
with *Nasi Kuning* (page 148).

Be siap mepanggang mesanten

grilled chicken with coconut milk sauce

I briefly deep-fry the pieces of leftover chicken from this dish the next day, and they become wonderfully crisp.

serves 4

1 chicken, about 1.5kg
2–3 tablespoons vegetable oil
salt and ground black pepper
1 lemongrass stalk
150g *Sambal Mbe* (page 156)
300ml thick coconut milk (page 184)
3 salam leaves
3 kaffir lime leaves

Halve the chicken lengthways. Rub both halves with the oil, salt and pepper. Grill for about 45 minutes over a hot charcoal fire or under the grill, until cooked through and golden brown. Cut the chicken halves into pieces and arrange them on a platter.

Trim the lemongrass, bruise the stalk and tie the leaves together in a knot.

Heat a dry wok and add the *sambal*, coconut milk, salam leaves, lime leaves and lemongrass. Bring to the boil and cook for 2–3 minutes, then pour the sauce over the chicken. Serve with *Nasi Kuning* (page 148).

Be siap guling

spit-roasted chicken

This chicken dish is derived from *Be Guling* (page 34) and is one of the best-known specialities of Bali.

serves 4

1 chicken, about 1.25kg
300g *Base Gede* (page 185)
3 salam leaves, very finely chopped
2–3 tablespoons vegetable oil
1 teaspoon ground turmeric

Stuff the chicken cavity with the *base gede* and salam leaves. Sew up the cavity with kitchen string. Fold the wings close to the body and secure with kitchen string.

Skewer the chicken on the turnspit and spit-roast for about 65 minutes in the oven or under the grill, until cooked and browned.

Mix the oil with the ground turmeric and use to baste the chicken regularly during roasting. Serve the chicken with the stuffing, white rice and *Sambal Mbe* (page 156).

Be siap mepanggang

roast chicken

A very popular dish during *odalan*, the birthday of the temple which is celebrated annually (according to the Balinese calendar every 210 days). It is accompanied by one of the most important religious ceremonies, involving everyone who is connected to the temple in one way or another.

Weeks before, the temple is cleaned and refurbished. When everything is spic and span, the priest invites the gods to come and take up residence in the temple for the duration of the ceremonies. In the meantime, the women start to make the decorations and offerings. In the early hours of the morning in which the ceremony is to be held, the men head to the temple to start preparing the food. When the women take their home-made offerings to the temple, everyone can see how artfully they have integrated spatchcocked roasted chicken in the towering offerings. These are offered to the gods and eaten at home afterwards. If the chicken is part of the pyramid offering, the dish is called *be siap mepanggang* (see photograph). Afterwards at home, it is often turned into *Be Siap Mesitsit* (page 68).

serves 2–3

1 chicken, about 1.25kg
5 tablespoons coconut oil
3 salam leaves
2 teaspoons salt

For the spice paste
7 candlenuts
5 shallots, peeled and
   finely sliced
7 garlic cloves, peeled and
   finely chopped
5 bird's eye chillies, sliced
2cm piece of fresh lesser
   galangal, peeled and
   finely chopped
4cm piece of fresh turmeric,
   peeled and finely chopped
5cm piece of fresh galangal,
   peeled and finely chopped
1 lemongrass stalk, very
   finely chopped
3 tablespoons melted *gula Bali*
   or palm sugar

Cut the chicken lengthways along the backbone. Press down firmly to flatten.

To make the spice paste, use a pestle and mortar to pound the candlenuts to a fine paste. Add the shallots, garlic, chillies, lesser galangal, turmeric, galangal, lemongrass and *gula Bali* or palm sugar and pound again to a paste.

Heat the coconut oil in a wok and fry the spice paste and salam leaves for 3 minutes. Remove from the heat and leave to cool.

Rub the chicken on the inside and outside with the spice paste and salt.

Grill the chicken for 50–55 minutes over a hot charcoal fire or under a hot grill, turning regularly, until brown and cooked through. Serve with white rice and *Sambal Tomat* (page 159).

Be siap mepanggang pelecing

grilled chicken with *sambal pelecing*

For the preparation of *sambal* and spice pastes the Balinese use a *cobek*. This is a flat mortar with a pounder or pestle made of natural stone. Before using a new *cobek*, it needs to be thoroughly rinsed with water (cold or warm), scrubbing with a stiff brush at the same time. Take some salt, add some water to it and pulverise it over the *cobek* with the *ulekan* (pounder or pestle). If the salt remains white, both the *cobek* and *ulekan* can be used in the kitchen straightaway. If it stays dark, repeat the salt treatment. If the salt is still dark after four or five rubbings, either the *cobek* or *ulekan*, or indeed both, are not fit for use in the kitchen. The maintenance of a *cobek* is very simple. After each use simply rinse it with cold or warm water, with no detergent, and leave to dry.

serves 4

1 chicken, about 1.25kg
4 tablespoons vegetable oil
salt
150g *sambal pelecing* (page 162)

Halve the chicken lengthways and rub both halves with 2 tablespoons oil and some salt. Grill the chicken for about 45 minutes over a hot charcoal fire or under a hot grill, until brown and cooked through. Cut the cooked chicken into small pieces.

Heat the remainder of the oil in a wok and fry the *sambal pelecing* for about 3 minutes.

Mix the cooked chicken pieces with the sambal. Serve with rice and *kangkung mepelecing* (page 132).

Be siap mesitsit
spicy chicken strips

serves 4

1 quantity *Be Siap Mepanggang*
   (page 64)
1 tablespoon vegetable oil
juice of 3 leprous limes
   (if unavailable, use kaffir
   limes)
salt

For the sauce

5 shallots, peeled and
   finely sliced
3 garlic cloves, peeled and
   finely chopped
3 long red chillies, deseeded
   and sliced
1 teaspoon roasted shrimp paste
1 beefsteak tomato, cut into
   small pieces

Grill the chicken according to the recipe for *Be Siap Mepanggang*. Pull the chicken meat off the bone and cut the meat and skin into narrow strips.

Heat the oil in a wok and fry the sauce ingredients for about 5 minutes.

Stir the chicken meat, lime juice and a little salt into the sauce. Serve with *Nasi Putih*, *Sambal Tomat* and *Jukut Urap* (pages 147, 159 and 128).

Cakep siap

chicken thighs steamed in banana leaf

During my cooking demonstrations, I always urge those present to be extremely careful when preparing *rawit* chillies (bird's eye chillies) and *lombok* chillies (long red chillies). Capsaicin, the active compound which causes the burning, prickling and hot sensation in the mouth, sticks to the fingers and hands and can irritate small wounds on them. Even washing with soap does not always remove capsaicin from the skin, and accidentally rubbing one's eyes can have very painful consequences. On Bali, it is customary to rub fingers and hands with a little oil before preparing chilli peppers. This prevents the capsaicin from sticking to the skin and it can be removed quickly with soap and water.

serves 4

4 chicken thighs, boned
5 tablespoons coconut oil
4 salam leaves

For the spice paste
1 teaspoon black peppercorns
3 shallots, peeled and
   finely sliced
3 garlic cloves, peeled and
   finely chopped
3 long red chillies, deseeded
   and sliced
7 bird's eye chillies, sliced
5cm piece of fresh ginger,
   peeled and finely chopped
3cm piece of fresh lesser
   galangal, peeled and
   finely chopped
4cm piece of fresh turmeric,
   peeled and finely chopped
2 tablespoons melted *gula Bali*
   or palm sugar
salt

banana leaves, washed
   and patted dry
bamboo strips or toothpicks

To make the spice paste, use a pestle and mortar to pound the peppercorns to a fine powder. Add the shallots, garlic, chillies, ginger, lesser galangal, turmeric and *gula Bali* or palm sugar and pound to a paste. Season with salt.

Cut each chicken thigh in half and mix the pieces with the spice paste and coconut oil. Cover and marinate for about 20 minutes in the fridge.

Cut four squares from the banana leaves, each about 20 x 20cm. On each one, place two pieces of chicken and one salam leaf. Make a parcel with the leaves and secure with bamboo strips or toothpicks.

Put the parcels in a steamer, ensuring they rest above the water. Cover and steam until cooked through, 40–45 minutes. Serve with white rice.

Cran cam

clear chicken soup

This is the tastiest chicken soup I know, and it is one of the many recipes my mother gave to me. For a long time she ran her own restaurant on Bali where she served local dishes. When, much later, I opened my own restaurant in Amsterdam, she came over to the Netherlands to help. Of course, I regularly asked her to prepare *cran cam* for my guests, and every time she made it she received enthusiastic compliments.

serves 4–6

1 lemongrass stalk
1 litre water
300g boneless, skinless
   chicken breasts
5 salam leaves
2 tablespoons *Base Megenep*
   (page 185)
salt
12–15 tablespoons vegetable oil
2 shallots, peeled and
   thinly sliced
leaves from 2 sprigs of Asian
   celery, finely chopped

Trim the lemongrass, bruise the stalk and tie the leaves together in a knot. In a pan, bring the water to the boil. Add the chicken breasts, lemongrass, salam leaves, *base megenep* and salt, and simmer for about 15 minutes. Strain the broth and set aside. Slice the chicken into strips.

Heat the oil in a wok and deep-fry the shallots until golden and crisp. Using a slotted spoon, transfer them to kitchen paper and leave to drain.

Divide the chicken strips between soup bowls and pour over the broth. Sprinkle with the deep-fried shallots and celery leaves and serve immediately.

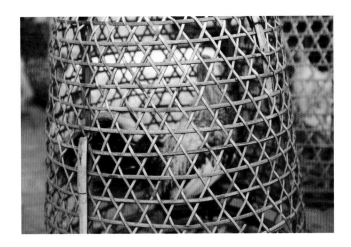

Pindang siap
chicken with *pindang* sauce

I was born on Bali and spent my youth there, but have now been living in Europe for over 25 years. Luckily, I do not get the chance to become homesick because I go home two to three times a year. But I do feel a little homesick every time I eat a typical Balinese dish, such as *pindang siap*, in Europe.

serves 4

1 litre water
7 kaffir lime leaves, very
   finely sliced
2 lemongrass stalks
1 chicken, about 1.25kg
150g *Base Gede* (page 185)
salt

Bring the water to the boil in a pan. Add the lime leaves and simmer gently until the water turns green.

Trim the lemongrass, bruise the stalks and tie the leaves together in a knot. Cut the chicken into eight pieces.

Add the *base gede*, chicken pieces and lemongrass to the water and simmer for about 35 minutes until the chicken is cooked. Serve with white rice.

Sate pajegan
minced chicken satay

There are plenty of satays in Balinese cuisine. When most tourists to Bali visit the *pasar malam* (the evening markets held all over the island), they notice there is much more on offer than merely *sateh ayam, sateh babi,* or *sateh kambing.* There is enormous variety in satays on Bali, and they are all freshly roasted at the *pasar malam,* and at the multitude of satay stalls on the sides of the roads. It is such a delight to eat them with a tasty sauce straight from the banana leaf!

makes about 30/serves 6

500g minced chicken
salt

For the spice paste
5 candlenuts
1 teaspoon coriander seeds
½ teaspoon ground cumin
1 teaspoon black peppercorns
3 shallots, peeled and
   finely sliced
3 garlic cloves, peeled and
   finely chopped
3 long red chillies, deseeded
   and sliced
5 bird's eye chillies, sliced
2cm piece of fresh ginger, peeled
   and finely chopped
2cm piece of fresh turmeric,
   peeled and finely chopped
2cm piece of fresh galangal,
   peeled and finely chopped
3 kaffir lime leaves, very
   finely chopped

about 30 flat, wide satay sticks

To make the spice paste, use a pestle and mortar to pound the candlenuts, coriander, cumin and peppercorns to a fine paste. Add the shallots, garlic, chillies, ginger, turmeric and galangal and pound again to a paste. Stir in the lime leaves.

Mix the minced chicken with the spice paste, and season with salt. Using your hands, shape a heaped tablespoon of the mixture into a ball, and mould it onto a satay stick. Repeat until the mince mixture is used up, about 30 satays.

Grill the satays for about 6 minutes over a hot charcoal fire or under a hot grill. Serve with white rice.

Sate pusut siap

sweet chicken satay

Connoisseurs of Indonesian cuisine all know that *gula Jawa* is more generally known as palm sugar. As the name implies, *gula Bali* is the Balinese version of this sugar. The sugar is harvested out of the thick and fibrous flower stalks of the *aren*, or sugar palm. A few days before the flower buds of these palms open, the stalks are bruised. Then the flower buds are cut off and a bunch of them are tied up with one of the stalks. At the point where the buds have been cut the stalks are rubbed with finely ground onion. This stimulates the flow of the *aren* juice. As soon as the flow is established, the cutting surface is cleaned and the juice is collected in a bamboo container. The juice is then turned into *gula Bali*.

makes about 30/serves 6

12–15 tablespoons vegetable oil
7 shallots, peeled and
  thinly sliced
500g minced chicken
salt
75ml thick coconut milk
  (page 184)
juice of 2 leprous limes
  (if unavailable, use kaffir limes)
3 tablespoons melted *gula
  Bali* or palm sugar

For the spice paste
2 garlic cloves, peeled and
  finely chopped
5 bird's eye chillies, sliced
3cm piece of fresh turmeric,
  peeled and finely chopped

about 30 flat, wide satay sticks

To make the spice paste, use a pestle and mortar to pound the garlic, chillies and turmeric to a fine paste.

Heat the oil in a wok and deep-fry the shallots until golden and crisp. Using a slotted spoon, transfer them to kitchen paper and leave to drain.

Mix the minced chicken with the spice paste, a little salt, the fried shallots, coconut milk, lime juice and melted *gula Bali* or palm sugar.

Using your hands, shape a heaped tablespoon of the mixture into a ball and mould it onto a satay stick. Repeat until the mixture is used up, about 30 satays.

Grill the satays for about 6 minutes over a hot charcoal fire or under a hot grill, until brown and cooked through. Serve with white rice.

Tum siap

spicy minced chicken in banana leaf

This is an authentic Balinese dish which I turned into a successful starter at my Amsterdam restaurant. *Tum siap* has a pronounced spicy flavour which pleases a lot of people. The fact that this dish is served in banana leaf makes it even more attractive!

makes 20/serves 5–6

12–15 tablespoons vegetable oil
1 shallot, peeled and thinly sliced
1 garlic clove, peeled and
    thinly sliced
2½ tablespoons thick coconut milk
    (page 184)
500g minced chicken
salt
20 small salam leaves

For the spice paste
½ teaspoon roasted shrimp paste
¼ teaspoon black peppercorns
2 shallots, peeled and finely sliced
3 garlic cloves, peeled and
    finely chopped
1 long red chilli, deseeded and sliced
3 bird's eye chillies, sliced
1½cm piece of fresh ginger, peeled
    and finely chopped
½cm piece of fresh lesser galangal,
    peeled and finely chopped
1½cm piece of fresh turmeric,
    peeled and finely chopped
1cm piece of fresh galangal,
    peeled and finely chopped

banana leaves, washed and
    patted dry
bamboo strips or toothpicks

To make the spice paste, use a pestle and mortar to pound the shrimp paste and peppercorns to a fine paste. Add the shallots, garlic, chillies, ginger, lesser galangal, turmeric and galangal and pound again to a paste.

Heat the oil in a wok. Deep-fry the shallot and garlic separately until golden and crisp. Using a slotted spoon, transfer them to kitchen paper and leave to drain.

Pour all but 3 tablespoons of the oil out of the wok, add the spice paste and stir-fry for about 3 minutes. Add the coconut milk and boil until the liquid has almost completely evaporated. Remove the wok from the heat and set aside to cool.

Mix the minced chicken with the cooled spice paste, shallot, garlic and a little salt. Divide the mixture into 20 portions.

Cut 20 pieces of banana leaf, each about 15 x 20cm. Place one salam leaf on each piece and top with a portion of chicken mixture. Fold both sides of the leaf over the filling. Fold the open ends over and secure the parcels with bamboo strips or toothpicks. Trim the empty ends at an angle to form a point at either end of the parcel.

Put the parcels into a steamer, ensuring they rest above the water. Steam until cooked through, about 25 minutes. Serve with white rice, *Sambal Mbe* and *Jukut Urap* (pages 156 and 128).

Bebek betutu

spicy duck roasted in palm leaves

After *Be Guling* (page 34), this duck dish is the best-known dish from the authentic Balinese kitchen. Of course, there are several versions of this dish. This recipe was given to me by Pak I Ketut Rimpi from Ubud, who has made the preparation of *bebek betutu* for feast days his profession, and I think this is the most original version. He wraps the duck in palm leaves, which are hard to find outside of Asia (if they are unobtainable, you can replace them with banana leaves). Because the leaves burn quickly in the oven, I usually use five layers. During the roasting, I occasionally peel off any burnt leaves.

Instead of duck, you can also use chicken (*ayam betutu*) for this dish, but the roasting time will be shorter.

makes 10–12/serves 5–6

2 ducks, each about 2kg,
  ready to cook
300g *Base Gede* (page 185)
6 salam leaves, finely chopped

For the marinade
2 teaspoons dried shrimp paste
1 tablespoon tamarind pulp
2 tablespoons *kecap asin*
100ml coconut oil
100ml water
2 teaspoons salt

2 palm leaves
bamboo strips or toothpicks

Preheat the oven to 200°C/400°F/gas mark 6.

In a bowl, mix together the ingredients for the marinade. Place the ducks in a dish and pour over the marinade. Massage them until the legs are supple enough to fold into the stomach cavity. Remove the ducks and reserve the marinade.

Divide the *base gede* and salam leaves into two portions and stuff one portion into the cavity of each duck. Mix the remaining portion with the marinade.

Place each duck on the bottom part of a palm leaf in an oven dish. Pour the marinade over, fold the leaf around the duck and secure with bamboo or toothpicks.

Roast the ducks for 1½–2 hours, turning the heat down to 150°C/300°F/gas mark 2 after 15 minutes of cooking. Serve with *Nasi Putih* and *Jukut Urap* (pages 147 and 128).

the traditional method

Covering an area of 50 x 50cm, pile bricks on top of each other until they stand half a metre high. Place the duck parcels on top. Cover them with a thick layer of rice husks so that they are completely covered.

Light the edges and the top of the rice husks with a match. The fire will slowly smoulder. Cook the ducks for about 11 hours until cooked through.

Bebek mekuah manis lalah

duck with a hot and sweet sauce

Most of the foreigners in Bali have come from Western countries, where sweet Asian dishes are very popular. This dish is always number one on the menus of those restaurants visited by foreigners.

serves 4

1 duck, about 1.5kg
3 lemongrass stalks
12–15 tablespoons vegetable oil
7 shallots, peeled and
  thinly sliced
150g *Base Megenep* (page 185)
9 cardamom pods
2 tablespoons melted *gula Bali* or
  palm sugar
2 tablespoons white wine vinegar
300ml boiling water
300ml thick coconut milk
  (page 184)
7 green bird's eye chillies, split
  open lengthways
salt
2 sprigs of Asian celery

Cut the duck into 8 pieces. Trim the lemongrass, bruise the stalks and tie the leaves together in a knot.

Heat the oil in a wok and deep-fry the shallots until golden and crisp. Using a slotted spoon, transfer them to kitchen paper and leave to drain.

Pour all but 3 tablespoons of the oil out of the wok and fry the *base megenep* and cardamom pods for about 3 minutes. Add the lemongrass and the duck pieces and stir-fry for about 3 minutes. Add the *gula Bali* or palm sugar, vinegar and boiling water. Simmer for about 1 hour until the duck is cooked through and the liquid has evaporated.

Add the coconut milk and chillies, season with salt and simmer for a further 5 minutes.

Take the celery leaves off the stems and sprinkle them over the duck. Sprinkle with the deep-fried shallots and serve with *Nasi Kuning* (page 148).

Sate pusut bebek

duck breast satay

Tourists regularly tell me that Balinese duck dishes have such a different taste from anything they are used to at home. The deeper flavour of the duck is not just the result of the herbs and spices used in the preparation, but also a result of the ducks on Bali growing up in the midst of nature and therefore eating only 'healthy' food. The ducks keep the rice paddies weed-free, and eat everything nature has to offer them in that environment so abundant with water. In other parts of the world, duck comes from special farms with less 'natural' food on the menu, which of course influences the taste of the meat.

makes about 30/serves 6

6 tablespoons vegetable oil
7 shallots, peeled and thinly sliced
1 teaspoon salt
50ml thick coconut milk (page 184)
1 teaspoon leprous lime juice (if
  unavailable, use kaffir lime)
3 tablespoons melted *gula Bali*
  or palm sugar
500g minced duck

about 30 flat, wide satay sticks

For the spice paste
3 garlic cloves, peeled and
  finely chopped
3cm piece of fresh turmeric,
  peeled and finely chopped
5 bird's eye chillies, sliced

Heat the oil in a wok and fry the shallots until golden.

To make the spice paste, use a pestle and mortar to pound the garlic, turmeric and chillies to a fine paste. Mix the spice paste with the fried shallots, salt, coconut milk, lime juice, melted *gula Bali* or palm sugar and minced duck.

Using your hands, shape a tablespoon of the mixture into a ball and mould it onto a satay stick. Repeat with the remaining mixture until it is used up, about 30 satays.

Grill the satays for about 8 minutes over a hot charcoal fire or under a hot grill, until brown and cooked through. Serve with white rice.

spicy minced duck in banana leaf

The name of this dish seems to imply a great similarity with *Tum Siap* (page 76), which is prepared with minced chicken meat. Yet the flavour of *tum bebek* is quite different because of the different ingredients used in this recipe. Both *tum siap* and *tum bebek* make attractive starters. Because of the totally different tastes of these dishes, they can be served together.

serves 4

600g duck breast, very
   finely chopped
1 teaspoon finely ground
   black pepper
150g *Sambal Mbe* (page 156)
2 tablespoons vegetable oil
2 tablespoons *Base Megenep*
   (page 185)
3 tablespoons coconut milk
   (page 184)
1 teaspoon salt

banana leaves, washed and
   patted dry
bamboo strips or toothpicks

In a bowl, mix the duck with the pepper, *sambal mbe*, oil, *base megenep*, coconut milk and salt.

Cut 25–30 pieces of banana leaf, each about 10 x 12cm. Place a heaped tablespoon of mixture on each leaf. Fold both sides of the leaf over the filling. Fold the open ends over and secure the parcels with bamboo strips or toothpicks.

Place the parcels in a steamer, ensuring they rest above the water. Steam until cooked through, about 20 minutes. Serve with white rice.

Teluh base lalah

fried hard-boiled eggs with spicy coconut sauce

This is one of the very few known egg dishes in Balinese cooking. I was always told that in the distant past, eggs were hardly eaten. Chicken and duck eggs were left to hatch to ensure there was always sufficient chicken and duck meat for offerings in the various temple ceremonies. Egg consumption has grown, though, since the establishment of chicken farms on Bali.

serves 4–6

6 eggs
6 tablespoons vegetable oil

For the spicy coconut sauce
2 tablespoons *Base Megenep*
   (page 185)
1 teaspoon *Base Wangenan*
   (page 185)
300ml thick coconut milk
   (page 184)
1 salam leaf
juice of 1 leprous lime
   (if unavailable, use kaffir lime)

Hard-boil the eggs for about 10 minutes, then plunge them into cold water and peel them.

Heat the oil in a wok and fry the whole, peeled eggs until golden brown.

Pour all but 2 tablespoons of the oil out of the wok and fry the *base megenep* for about 3 minutes. Add the *base wangenan*, coconut milk, salam leaf and lime juice and simmer for 1 minute. Add the eggs, coat with the sauce and simmer for a further 5 minutes before serving.

Teluh mesambel goreng

fried hard-boiled eggs
with *sambal megoreng*

This egg dish has similarities with *Teluh Base Lalah* (page 82). The basic preparation is identical, but the sauce is made up of completely different ingredients, resulting in a flavour quite distinct from the other dish. In fact, they are dissimilar enough for me to make both when I am cooking a large spread.

serves 4–6

6 eggs
6 tablespoons vegetable oil
5 shallots, peeled and
  thinly sliced
3cm piece of fresh galangal,
  peeled and finely chopped
3 salam leaves
150g *Sambal Megoreng* (page 158)

Hard-boil the eggs for about 10 minutes, then plunge them into cold water and peel them.

Heat the oil in a wok and fry the eggs until light brown. Remove them from the wok along with all but 3 tablespoons of the oil. Add the shallots and stir-fry for about 2 minutes. Add the galangal, salam leaves and *sambal megoreng* and simmer briefly.

Halve the eggs lengthways and arrange them on a platter. Pour over the *sambal megoreng*. Serve with white rice.

Fish and seafood

Bali is completely surrounded by water, so it is natural that tourists would expect to find a lot of fish dishes. They are regularly disappointed, however. On religious grounds, fish is of secondary importance on Bali. According to the Hindu faith, the gods, holy beings and ancestors live above the ground and have taken possession of the heavens. When they descend, they dwell in mountains. When they leave the heavens, most of the gods take up residence in the Pura Besakih, the mother temple which has been erected on the slopes of the Gunung Besakih. Shiva, the highest god, has his own seat there. The belief that the gods dwell in the mountains has led the Balinese to believe that all good things come from these mountains.

To the gods, the earth consists only of their island Bali. And then there is the sea, which lies beneath the level of the earth. This is the dwelling of demons and monsters. The sea therefore inspires fear and is also considered unclean. For centuries, this kept the Balinese from indulging in eating fish and other fruits of the sea. The coral reef close to the coast also made fishing very difficult, acting as a vast barrier to the tiny fishing vessels. Fish has always been inferior food, eaten mainly by the poor, and it is still much cheaper than meat. However, over the years the supply has become larger and more varied, in part due to the tourists, who greatly appreciate fish and shellfish dishes. And though the locals now take a more positive attitude towards this food, the fear of the sea has remained constant. A Balinese who makes a living as a fisherman and takes a small boat out to sea in all weather conditions in the hope of returning with a rich harvest is considered to be a truly brave man. The number of fishermen has increased over recent years, with the discovery that fish can be a lucrative business. When the Balinese want to catch fish, they prefer to use a rod and net from the safety of the reef or beach, so that they do not lose contact with the earth.

The waters surrounding Bali guarantee a plentiful daily supply of fish and, in spite of its lack of popularity among the locals, each market now offers a rich choice of fish and seafood. The main catch consists of mackerel, sardines, tuna, red snapper and octopus. Because of its limited storage life, most fish is first dried on the beach in the sun, then taken to market for retail. Fish is also salted or put in brine to prolong storage time.

The explosion in tourism has led to a dramatic increase in different kinds of fish and shellfish pulled from the sea. Large crabs, king prawns, shrimp and lobsters are caught daily and appear proudly on the menus of the many restaurants.

Be pasih megoreng base lalah

fried fish with chilli sauce

Most Balinese fishermen use slender boats fitted with two characteristic 'wings', there to help prevent the boats from colliding with each other. They go to sea every evening and do not return until dawn the following day. Nine day breaks, called *bulan terang*, are often observed; three days before the full moon and extending a further six days. There is no fishing during this time, because it is generally believed that the sardines can see the nets by the moonlight and will swim away. Also, because of the shimmering moonlight on the water, the fishermen have difficulty catching the schools of sardines. These short intervals are used to repair their boats and nets.

serves 4

1 medium-sized fish,
   about 1kg, such as red
   snapper
2 garlic cloves, peeled and
   finely chopped
400ml vegetable oil
salt
500ml thick coconut milk
   (page 184)

For the spice paste
5 candlenuts
1 teaspoon dried shrimp
   paste
7 shallots, peeled and
   finely sliced
3 garlic cloves, peeled and
   finely chopped
5 long red chillies, sliced
9 bird's eye chillies, sliced

To make the spice paste, use a pestle and mortar to pound the candlenuts and shrimp paste to a fine paste. Add the shallots, garlic and chillies and pound again to a paste.

Rinse the fish, pat dry and rub inside and out with garlic, oil and some salt.

Heat 3 tablespoons of the oil in a wok and fry the spice paste for about 3 minutes. Add the coconut milk and a little salt and simmer until the sauce thickens.

Heat the rest of the oil in a frying pan and fry the fish for about 15 minutes on each side until golden and cooked through. Pour the sauce over the fried fish and serve with white rice.

Be tongkol megoreng sambal matah

fried tuna with fresh *sambal*

The waters around Bali contain different kinds of tuna, varying in weight from 3 to 5kg, and in length from 0.5 to 1.5m long – they are all suitable for use in this recipe. The most well-known is the Eastern little tuna or wavy-backed skipjack. In the Balinese markets, these tunas are usually sold already cut into thick steaks.

serves 4–6

500g fresh tuna fillet
6 tablespoons vegetable oil
150g *Sambal Matah* (page 155)
freshly ground black pepper

For the marinade
5 candlenuts
1 teaspoon dried shrimp paste
2 teaspoons sugar
4cm piece of fresh ginger, peeled
   and finely chopped
1 teaspoon tamarind pulp

To make the marinade, use a pestle and mortar to pound the candlenuts, shrimp paste and sugar to a fine paste. Add the ginger and tamarind and pound again to a paste. Add the tuna to the marinade and leave to soak up the flavours for about 15 minutes. Remove the tuna.

Heat the oil in a wok and fry the tuna quickly on each side until golden. Remove the fish from the wok and mix it with the *sambal matah* and black pepper.

Serve with white rice and *Kangkung Mepelecing* (page 132).

Be pindang megoreng

fried salted sardines

The majority of caught fish are sardines, and the largest catches occur on the south-west coast: Pengambengan and Kedonganan are the two best-known fishing villages. Early every morning, merchants gather on the beach to purchase the fishermen's catch. Salted sardines (pictured opposite) are sold at the marketplace in woven baskets.

serves 4

300ml vegetable oil
12 salted sardines
3 tablespoons *Sambal Tomat*
   (page 159)

Heat the oil in a wok and fry the sardines on each side until golden and cooked through. Using a slotted spoon, remove to a plate lined with kitchen paper.

Pour all but 3 tablespoons of the oil out of the wok, add the *sambal tomat* and stir-fry for about 3 minutes. Stir in the sardines and serve with white rice.

Lindung mekuah

soup with sawa eel

Only sea salt is used in Balinese cuisine. It has always been a cheap ingredient provided by nature to the island inhabitants. Bali has many small family businesses situated on the beaches, extracting salt from sea water collected in shallow basins. When the water evaporates in the hot sun, the salt is left behind.

serves 4

5 sawa eels
12–15 tablespoons vegetable oil
5 shallots, peeled and
   finely sliced
500ml chicken stock
3 green chillies, deseeded
   and sliced
1 tablespoon *Base Megenep*
   (page 185)
salt

Clean the eels and cut them into pieces about 3cm long.

Heat the oil in a wok. Deep-fry the shallots until golden and crisp. Using a slotted spoon, remove the shallots to kitchen paper and leave to drain.

Meanwhile, bring the stock to the boil, add the pieces of eel and simmer for about 10 minutes on a low heat until tender. Add the chillies and *base megenep*. Season with salt and simmer for a further 5 minutes.

Sprinkle the fried shallots over the soup and serve.

Bulung kuah pindang

seaweed with *pindang* sauce

Kuah pindang is a well-known condiment on Bali. It is a fish sauce made from the sieved liquid in which fish has been soaked for several days. It has a strong and penetrating odour and flavour, but is not overbearing when mixed with the right ingredients.

serves 4–6

500g fine seaweed

For the *pindang* sauce
2 teaspoons roasted dried
    shrimp paste
1 teaspoon dry-roasted bird's eye
    chilli, coarsely ground
5 bird's eye chillies, sliced
200ml *pindang* water (page 189)
salt

Wash the seaweed and drain well.

To make the *pindang* sauce, pound the shrimp paste and dry-roasted bird's eye chilli together. Add the bird's eye chillies, and stir the mixture into the *pindang* water. Season with salt.

Arrange the seaweed on a platter and pour over the *pindang* sauce.

Pepes base barak

spicy fish in banana leaf

I was brought up eating chillies, but I can imagine that some people might be shocked at the amount of chilli used in Balinese cooking. This fish recipe is traditionally a hot dish, but check the number of bird's eye chillies in the spice paste. If you prefer a milder version, simply use fewer chillies. On Bali, skipjack tuna is used for this dish, but cod is also suitable.

serves 4

500g cod fillet
3 tablespoons vegetable oil
salt
4 salam leaves

For the spice paste
5 shallots, peeled and
    finely sliced
3 long red chillies, deseeded
    and sliced
15 bird's eye chillies, sliced
2 teaspoons dried shrimp paste
5cm piece of fresh ginger, peeled
    and finely chopped

banana leaves, rinsed
    and patted dry
bamboo strips or toothpicks

Rinse the cod fillet, pat it dry and cut it into small pieces.

To make the spice paste, use a pestle and mortar to pound the shallots, chillies, shrimp paste and ginger to a fine paste.

Coat the fish with the spice paste and some oil, and season with salt.

Cut four squares of banana leaf, each about 25cm. Place one salam leaf on each square and top with a quarter of the fish mixture. Fold both sides of the leaf over the filling. Fold the open ends over and secure the parcels with bamboo strips or toothpicks.

Place the parcels in a steamer, ensuring they rest above the water. Steam the parcels for about 15 minutes. Just before serving, place over a charcoal fire or under a hot grill for 2–3 minutes each side, then serve immediately with white rice.

Gerang

deep-fried salted fish

Baruna, the goddess of the sea, is praised and honoured daily, in order to gain her favour and protection from the demons living in the sea. Fishermen's wives put home-made offerings in the prows of their husbands' boats to show respect for the goddess, and to ask for her assistance in bringing their husbands home safely.

serves 3–4

350g dried salted fish
  (*ikan teri* – page 187)
3 shallots, peeled and
  finely sliced
3 garlic cloves, peeled
  and thinly sliced
5 bird's eye chillies, sliced
2cm piece of fresh lesser
  galangal, peeled and
  finely chopped

1 teaspoon roasted dried
  shrimp paste
1 teaspoon *gula Bali* or
  palm sugar
400ml coconut oil
1 tomato, cut into wedges
1 salam leaf
salt

Soak the fish in cold water for 20 minutes. Drain, rinse and pat dry.

Using a pestle and mortar, pound the shallots, garlic, chillies, lesser galangal, shrimp paste and *gula Bali* or palm sugar to a paste.

Heat the coconut oil in a wok and deep-fry the fish until crisp. Using a slotted spoon, remove to a plate lined with kitchen paper.

Pour all but 3 tablespoons of the oil from the wok. Reheat until hot, add the spice paste, tomato and salam leaf and fry for about 3 minutes. Add the fried fish and stir-fry for a further 1 minute. Season with salt and serve with white rice.

Ikan mepanggang sambal matah

grilled fish with fresh *sambal*

Under the great smoke of the international airport Ngurah Rai, on southern Bali, in a picturesque inlet, lies the fishing village Jimbaran. Years ago, in the evening, I used to go to the beach where fishermen who wanted to earn some extra money would set up tables and chairs and serve up fresh fish. Since then, tourists have discovered Jimbaran and the beach is now almost entirely covered with beach huts and small restaurants. Evenings there are full of activity, but what has not changed is the quality of the food. I still enjoy *ikan mepanggang* with *sambal matah* and there is nowhere in the world you can get it fresher.

serves 4

1 medium-sized fish, about 1kg,
  such as red snapper

For the spice paste
5 garlic cloves, peeled
  and finely chopped
6cm piece of fresh turmeric,
  peeled and finely chopped
juice of 1 lime
3 tablespoons coconut oil
salt

Wash the fish and pat it dry.

To make the spice paste, use a pestle and mortar to pound the garlic and turmeric to a fine paste. Mix in the lime juice, coconut oil and a little salt. Rub this mixture on the outside and the inside of the fish.

Grill the fish for about 20 minutes (10 minutes on each side) over a charcoal fire or under a hot grill until brown and cooked through.

Serve with *sambal matah* (page 155), white rice and *Kangkung Mepelecing* (page 132).

Lempet tongkol

spicy fish grilled in banana leaf

A dish that you will find nowhere else, *lempet tongkol* is always part of offerings to the gods and ancestors on high days and holidays, such as weddings or the feast in honour of teeth filing. Teeth filing is an important part of the lifecycle of every Balinese man and woman. Between the ages of 12 and 16 every boy and girl has to have their teeth filed. With this ceremony, they enter adulthood. This ceremony is an important way of ensuring each Balinese man and woman will be recognised by the gods in heaven. If a child dies before they have had their teeth filed, this ceremony will happen after their death.

makes 10/serves 3–4

500g fresh tuna fillet
100ml thick coconut milk
   (page 184)
salt

For the spice paste
3 shallots, peeled and
   finely sliced
3 garlic cloves, peeled
   and thinly sliced
1 long red chilli, deseeded
   and sliced
3 bird's eye chillies,
   deseeded and sliced
½ teaspoon roasted dried
   shrimp paste
1 tablespoon grated *gula
   Bali* or palm sugar
juice of 3 leprous limes
   (if unavailable, use kaffir limes)

banana leaves, washed
   and patted dry
bamboo strips or toothpicks

Cut half of the fish into small pieces and finely chop the remaining fillet.

For the spice paste, use a pestle and mortar to pound the shallots, garlic, chillies, shrimp paste, *gula Bali* or palm sugar and lime juice to a paste.

Combine the spice paste with the chopped fish and the fish pieces. Gradually stir in the coconut milk to make a stiff batter. Season with salt.

Cut 10 pieces from the banana leaves, each about 15 x 20cm. Place a portion of the fish mixture on each leaf. Fold both sides of the leaf over the filling. Fold the open ends over and secure the parcels with bamboo strips or toothpicks.

Grill the parcels for 10 minutes over a hot charcoal fire or under a hot grill. Serve with white rice.

Lindung goreng

deep-fried sawa eels

serves 3–4

1kg sawa eels (if unavailable,
   use elver eels)
2 teaspoons coriander seeds
1 teaspoon white peppercorns
5 garlic cloves, peeled and
   finely chopped
2cm piece of fresh lesser
   galangal, peeled and
   finely chopped
3cm piece of fresh turmeric,
   peeled and finely chopped
3 kaffir lime leaves, very
   finely chopped
250g rice flour
about 400ml water
salt
vegetable oil

The eels that thrive among the young plants in the paddy fields curl up
as soon as they go into the hot oil and therefore take on a completely
different appearance. They are tastiest when deep-fried until crisp. In many
of the marketplaces on Bali, they are deep-fried on the spot and eaten
immediately. Absolutely delicious!

Wash the eels well.

Using a pestle and mortar, crush the coriander seeds and peppercorns,
then add the garlic, lesser galangal and turmeric and pound to a paste.

Mix the spice paste with the lime leaves, rice flour and enough water to
make a thick, smooth batter. Season with salt. Heat plenty of oil in a
wok. Coat the eels with the batter and deep-fry until golden and crisp.

Pepes base Bali

fish with spices in banana leaf

This is the Balinese version of the celebrated Indonesian dish known as *pepes ikan*. The selection of herbs and spices gives this dish its distinct flavour and aroma. Panga is used on Bali but since this is mostly only found in the waters of Southeast Asia, you can substitute this with any other kind of white-fleshed fish.

serves 4–6

500g fish fillets
  such as cod, whiting or panga
1 sprig lemon basil
3 tablespoons *Base Megenep* (page 185)
3 kaffir lime leaves, finely sliced
1 tomato, sliced in wedges
1 tablespoon melted *gula Bali*
  or palm sugar
juice of 2 leprous limes
  (if unavailable, use kaffir limes)
salt

banana leaves, washed
  and patted dry
bamboo strips or toothpicks

Rinse the fillets, pat dry and cut into small pieces. Pick the leaves off the basil sprig.

Mix the fish with the *base megenep*, basil leaves, kaffir lime leaves, tomato, *gula Bali* or palm sugar, lime juice and salt.

Cut four 25 x 20cm pieces from the banana leaves. Place a quarter of the fish mixture on each leaf. Fold both sides of the leaf over the filling. Fold the open ends over and secure the parcels with bamboo strips or toothpicks.

Place the fish parcels briefly over a charcoal fire or under a hot grill until cooked through. Serve with white rice and *Sambal Mbe* (page 156).

Pindang ikan

fish in spicy sour sauce

Personally, I think this is the ideal fish dish with which to introduce someone to Balinese cuisine. It is not too hot, but it is spicy – just as dishes from this cuisine should be – with a tanginess from the kaffir lime leaves, lemongrass and salam leaves.

serves 4–6

7 kaffir lime leaves, very finely sliced
300ml water
750g white fish fillet, such as cod
1 lemongrass stalk

For the *base gede*
100g *Base Megenep* (page 185)
¾ teaspoon *Base Wangenan* (page 185)
1½ salam leaves

In a pan, bring the lime leaves and water to the boil, then reduce the heat and simmer gently until the water turns green.

Rinse the fish fillet, pat it dry and cut it into small pieces. Trim the lemongrass, bruise the stalk and tie the leaves together in a knot.

Mix all the ingredients for the *base gede* together, then stir it into the green water in the pan. Add the lemongrass and the pieces of fish and poach on a low heat for 15–20 minutes, stirring regularly.

Serve the fish with the sauce and *Nasi Kuning* (page 148).

Sager

grated coconut and whitebait salad

Take care when prising the flesh out of a coconut as it is not an easy job. Use a short-bladed knife to reduce the risk of the knife slipping. Desiccated coconut is an alternative, but I do find that using freshly grated coconut gives the best results. A good alternative to fresh is frozen grated coconut.

serves 6

100g fresh coconut flesh
    (about half a small coconut)
100g whitebait
400ml vegetable oil
125ml *Sambal Mbe* (page 156)
leaves from 2 sprigs of
    lemon basil

Remove the coconut flesh in large pieces from the shell and grill them over hot charcoal or under a grill until they colour. Remove the dark brown skin and coarsely grate the flesh.

Rinse the whitebait, drain it and pat it dry.

Heat the oil in a wok and deep-fry the whitebait until crisp. Drain on kitchen paper and when cool enough to handle, crumble the fish with your hands.

Combine the crumbled fish with the grated coconut, *sambal* and basil leaves. Serve with white rice.

Sate languan

spicy ground fish satay with coconut

This is one of the favourite satay versions on the island where I was born. As far as preparation goes, it resembles *Sate Lilit* (page 104). The flavour, however, is a little milder and is therefore always served on Bali with the hot and spicy *sambal mbe*. *Sate lilit* is a traditional dish that is often prepared for ceremonies, whilst *sate languan* is a more commonplace and homely dish. To prevent the satay sticks from catching during grilling, it is best to soak them first in cold water for about 30 minutes.

makes about 30/serves 4–6

500g white fish fillet
2 shallots, peeled and
    finely sliced
2 garlic cloves, peeled
    and finely chopped
2 long red chillies, deseeded
    and sliced
100g grated fresh coconut
300g *Sambal Mbe* (page 156)
75ml thick coconut milk
    (page 184)
½ tablespoon grated *gula Bali*
    or palm sugar
juice of 1 leprous lime
    (if unavailable, use a kaffir
    lime)
salt

flat, wide satay sticks

Rinse the fish fillet, pat it dry and chop very finely.

Use a pestle and mortar to pound the shallots, garlic and red chillies to a paste.

Mix the fish with the spice paste, grated coconut, *sambal*, coconut milk and *gula Bali* or palm sugar. Add the lime juice and season with salt.

Using your hands, shape small amounts of the fish mixture around the middle of a satay stick.

Grill over a charcoal fire or under a hot grill until brown and cooked through.

Palem kakul

grilled prawns and snails in banana leaf

The Balinese are said to eat everything that moves, and perhaps that was once the case. To get enough protein in their diets, people ate dragonflies, crickets, ants, lizards, hedgehogs, grubs and caterpillars; these were nature's bounty. Most Westerners would baulk at the idea of anything like that being served to them. Tourism has made the Balinese financially better off, which means they can afford to eat beef and pork more often. Snails, however, remain on the menu and are considered a delicacy.

serves 4

200g raw prawns
200g snails
2 tablespoons *Base Megenep*
  (page 185)
1 teaspoon ground coriander
1 tablespoon melted *gula Bali*
  or palm sugar
3 tablespoons coconut oil
salt
5 salam leaves

banana leaves, washed
  and patted dry
bamboo strips or toothpicks

Peel the prawns, rinse the snails and drain.

Mix the prawns and snails with the *base megenep*, coriander, *gula Bali* or palm sugar, coconut oil and a little salt. Cover and refrigerate for about 30 minutes.

Cut eight pieces from the banana leaves, each measuring about 20 x 25cm. Divide the prawn mixture into four. For each parcel, put 2 pieces of banana leaf on top of one another. Top with a salam leaf and then a quarter of the prawn mixture. Fold both sides of the leaf over the filling. Fold the open ends over and secure the parcels with bamboo strips or toothpicks.

Place the parcels in a steamer, cover and steam until tender, about 20 minutes. Serve with *Nasi Putih* (page 147).

Pepes telengis

spicy prawns
with coconut in banana leaf

I consider this a very special dish, all the more because it is very seldom made on Bali – possibly because of the time it takes to prepare. The coconut milk has to be boiled for an hour before the real preparation of the *pepes telengis* can begin. It is in danger of becoming a 'forgotten dish', and because it also has such an amazing flavour I felt I had to include it in this book. A dish to really surprise and spoil your guests with.

serves 4

500ml thick coconut milk
  (page 184)
sprig of lemon basil
1 tomato, cut into 8 wedges
250g large raw prawns, peeled
150g *Sambal Mbe* (page 156)
2 tablespoons tamarind pulp
7 salam leaves
1 tablespoon melted *gula Bali*
  or palm sugar
1 teaspoon finely ground
  white pepper

banana leaves, washed
  and patted dry
bamboo strips or toothpicks

Boil the coconut milk in a small pan for about 1 hour, until it is reduced to about 3 tablespoons (this is the *telengis*). Strip the leaves from the basil sprig.

Mix the *telengis* with the basil leaves, tomato, prawns, *sambal mbe*, tamarind pulp, salam leaves, *gula Bali* or palm sugar and pepper. Cover and refrigerate for 30 minutes.

Cut three squares, each about 30cm, from the banana leaves and stack them on top of one another. Pick the salam leaves out of the prawn mixture and put them on top of this. Place the prawn mixture in the middle. Fold both sides of the leaf over the filling. Fold the open ends over and secure the parcel with bamboo strips or toothpicks.

Put the parcel into a steamer, ensuring it rests above the water. Cover and steam until tender, about 20 minutes. Serve with white rice and *Sambal Mbe* (page 156).

'It is in danger of becoming a 'forgotten dish', and because it also has such an amazing flavour I felt I had to include it in this book.'

Pepes udang
prawns in banana leaf

For years I ran an Indonesian restaurant in Amsterdam, and because of my Balinese background there were, naturally, many special dishes from my homeland on the menu. *Pepes udang* was one of them and also one of the most popular prawn dishes. Not only is it a particularly delicious dish, but it is also a feast for the eyes. Before serving this to my guests, I would remove the bamboo strips and open up the leaves.

serves 4

500g raw prawns, peeled
salt
1 tomato, cut into wedges
3 kaffir lime leaves, cut into
   very fine strips
leaves from 3 sprigs of lemon basil
3 salam leaves

banana leaves, washed
   and patted dry
bamboo strips or toothpicks

For the spice paste

5 candlenuts
1 teaspoon coriander seeds
1 teaspoon dried shrimp paste
5 shallots, peeled and finely sliced
3 garlic cloves, peeled
   and finely chopped
5 long red chillies, deseeded
   and sliced
5 bird's eye chillies, sliced
3cm piece of fresh ginger,
   peeled and finely chopped
3cm piece of fresh turmeric,
   peeled and finely chopped
1 lemongrass stalk, finely chopped
2 teaspoons tamarind pulp

To make the spice paste, use a pestle and mortar to pound the candlenuts, coriander and shrimp paste to a fine paste. Add the shallots, garlic, chillies, ginger, turmeric, lemongrass and tamarind and pound again to a paste.

Wash the prawns and pat them dry. Put them in a bowl and add the spice paste with a little salt. Mix well, then stir in the tomato and lime leaves. Leave to marinate for 2 hours.

Cut a square, about 35–40cm, from the banana leaf. Place the basil and salam leaves on top. Place the prawn mixture in the middle. Fold both sides of the banana leaf over the filling. Fold the open ends over and secure the parcel with bamboo strips or toothpicks.

Put the parcel in a steamer, ensuring it rests above the water. Cover and steam until tender, about 15 minutes. If desired, place the *pepes* briefly over a charcoal fire or under a hot grill before serving with *Nasi Putih* (page 147).

Sate lilit

fish and prawn satay

This is exactly how my father taught me to make this dish, adding prawns to a satay normally made with just fish. On Bali, sate lilit is eaten mainly during temple ceremonies.

makes 20/serves 4

200g fish fillet, such as cod
  or beliga
200g raw prawns
5 bird's eye chillies, sliced
2 teaspoons black peppercorns
1 tablespoon *Base Megenep*
  (page 185)
1 teaspoon *Base Wangenan*
  (page 185)
5 kaffir lime leaves, very
  finely sliced
100g grated fresh coconut
100ml thick coconut milk
  (page 184)
3 tablespoons gula Bali or
  palm sugar
salt

20 wide satay sticks

Rinse the fish and prawns and pat them dry. Finely chop 200g of the fish together with the prawns. Slice the remaining fish into 20 even-sized slices.

Use a pestle and mortar to pound the chillies and peppercorns to a fine paste.

Mix the chopped fish and prawns with the chilli paste, *base megenep* and *wangenan*, lime leaves, grated coconut, coconut milk, gula Bali or palm sugar and a little salt. The mixture should be fairly stiff.

Thread the slices of fish lengthways onto the satay sticks and, using your hands, shape a tablespoon of the fish mixture around each one.

Grill the satays for about 5 minutes over a charcoal fire or under a hot grill, until brown and cooked through. Serve with white rice and *Jukut Urap* (page 128).

Udang bakar sambal matah
grilled king prawns with fresh *sambal*

Not only delicious, but also an extremely simple and healthy dish. If at all possible, I like to enjoy this dish at the fishing village Jimbaran, where just as with *Ikan Mepanggang* (page 93), it is made on the spot.

serves 4

12–16 raw king prawns, shells on

For the marinade
5 garlic cloves, peeled and
    finely chopped
6cm piece of fresh turmeric,
    peeled and finely chopped
juice of 1 lime
2 tablespoons coconut oil
salt

Rinse the prawns and pat them dry, but do not peel them.

To make the marinade, use a pestle and mortar to pound the garlic and turmeric to a fine paste. Add the lime juice, coconut oil and a little salt. Add the prawns and mix well to coat. Cover and leave to marinate for 30 minutes in a cool place.

Grill the prawns over a charcoal fire or under a hot grill for 2–3 minutes on each side, until cooked through.

Serve with 300g *sambal matah* together with *Nasi Sela* or *Nasi Ubi* (pages 155, 151 and 147).

Udang mesanten

king prawns with spicy coconut milk

'Is coconut milk the liquid inside a coconut?' I am asked this question at virtually every cookery demonstration or culinary workshop that I give. Coconut milk and coconut water are not the same thing. Coconut milk is made by soaking freshly grated coconut in tepid water then squeezing it out through a sieve placed above a bowl. Coconut water can be poured out of the shell after it has been cracked open. The water from a young coconut is often used to make exotic cocktails, and the water from older coconuts is perfect for marinating tough meat in order to tenderise it.

serves 4

500g raw king prawns, shells on
1 lemongrass stalk
sprig of lemon basil
5 tablespoons vegetable oil
5 shallots, peeled and
  thinly sliced
3 kaffir lime leaves
300ml thick coconut milk
  (page 184)
salt

For the spice paste
5 candlenuts
2 teaspoons roasted dried
  shrimp paste
1 teaspoon white peppercorns
1 teaspoon granulated sugar
3 garlic cloves, peeled and
  finely chopped
5 long red chillies, deseeded
  and sliced
7 bird's eye chillies, sliced
5cm piece of fresh ginger,
  peeled and finely chopped
3cm piece of fresh turmeric,
  peeled and finely chopped

To make the spice paste, use a pestle and mortar to pound the candlenuts, shrimp paste, peppercorns and sugar to a fine paste. Add the garlic, chillies, ginger and turmeric and pound again to a paste.

Peel the prawns, leaving the tail segments intact. Split them along the back and devein them, then rinse them and pat them dry. Trim the lemongrass, bruise the stalk and tie the leaves together in a knot. Strip the basil leaves from the sprig.

Heat the oil in a wok and add the shallots. Fry for 2 minutes, then add the spice paste, lemongrass and lime leaves. Fry for about 3 minutes, then add the coconut milk and season with salt.

Add the prawns and simmer for about 4 minutes until cooked through. Just before serving, add the lemon basil leaves. Serve with white rice.

'"Is coconut milk the liquid inside a coconut?" I am asked this question at virtually every cookery demonstration or culinary workshop that I give.'

Udang goreng
deep-fried prawns in batter

A coating of batter for certain ingredients is not originally a Balinese concept, but a result of the influence of Chinese cooking. However, the spices added are definitely Balinese!

serves 4–6

12–18 raw king prawns,
   shells on
3 tablespoons vegetable oil for
   frying the spice paste, and
   400ml for deep-frying
150g rice flour
2 kaffir lime leaves,
   cut into fine strips
salt

For the spice paste

1 teaspoon dried shrimp
   paste
2 teaspoons coriander seeds
2 shallots, peeled and
   finely sliced
3 garlic cloves, peeled
   and finely chopped
2 long red chillies, deseeded
   and sliced
2cm piece of fresh lesser
   galangal, peeled and
   finely chopped
2cm piece of fresh turmeric,
   peeled and finely chopped
2cm piece of fresh galangal,
   peeled and finely chopped

Peel the prawns, leaving the tail segment intact. Split them along the back and devein them.

To make the spice paste, use a pestle and mortar to pound the shrimp paste and coriander seeds to a fine paste. Add the shallots, garlic, chillies, lesser galangal, turmeric and galangal and pound again to a paste.

Heat 3 tablespoons of oil in a wok and fry the spice paste for about 3 minutes. Remove from the heat and leave to cool.

In a bowl, mix the rice flour with the cooled spice paste, lime leaves, a little salt and about 175ml water to make a smooth batter.

Heat the 400ml of oil in a wok for deep-frying. Holding a prawn by the tail, dip it in the batter to coat. Deep-fry the prawns five at a time for about 3 minutes, until golden. Drain on kitchen paper and keep them warm while you fry the remaining prawns. Serve hot with *Nasi Kuning* and *Sambal Megoreng* (pages 148 and 158).

Kakul mekuah

snails in spicy broth

This dish brings back childhood memories for me – as children we always found eating tiny snails very exciting. You had to suck the meat out of the shells and when you did, nine times out of ten, the meat of course would shoot right into your throat. It was so slippery that my brothers, sisters and I found this 'soup' great fun to eat!

serves 4

48 small snails
2 teaspoons tamarind pulp
1 lemongrass stalk
2 tablespoons vegetable oil
1 litre boiling water
salt
5 salam leaves

For the spice paste
7 candlenuts
1 teaspoon coriander seeds
1 teaspoon roasted dried
  shrimp paste
1 teaspoon white peppercorns
1 teaspoon black peppercorns
7 shallots, peeled and
  finely sliced
3 garlic cloves, peeled
  and finely chopped
7 bird's eye chillies, sliced
5cm piece of fresh ginger, peeled
  and finely chopped
6cm piece of fresh turmeric,
  peeled and finely chopped

To make the spice paste, use a pestle and mortar to pound the candlenuts, coriander, shrimp paste and peppercorns to a fine paste. Add the shallots, garlic, chillies, ginger and turmeric and pound again to a paste.

Rinse the snails and drain them. If necessary, remove the pips from the tamarind pulp. Cut off and discard the upper part of the lemongrass stalk. Slice the stalk and bruise the pieces using the side of a heavy knife.

Heat the oil in a wok and fry the spice paste for about 3 minutes. Add the water and season with salt. Add the snails, tamarind, lemongrass and salam leaves and simmer for about 20 minutes. Serve with white rice.

Udang pelalah

fried spicy king prawns

In the many restaurants in Sanur, Kuta and also in Lovina in the north, you will always find this prawn dish on the menu – on Bali, prawns are not very expensive, and many tourists consider them a delicacy. I always find this a very popular dish with guests. I think it's because the sweet flavour of the prawns is offset by the fresh and slightly tangy flavour of the lemongrass, lime juice and tamarind.

serves 4

500g raw king prawns, peeled
1 lemongrass stalk
2 tablespoons vegetable oil
3 salam leaves
juice of 3 leprous limes
    (if unavailable, use kaffir limes)
200ml thick coconut milk
    (page 184)
2 teaspoons tamarind pulp
granulated sugar
salt

For the spice paste
5 candlenuts
1 teaspoon roasted dried
    shrimp paste
5 shallots, peeled and
    finely sliced
3 garlic cloves, peeled
    and finely chopped
3 long red chillies, deseeded
    and sliced
11 bird's eye chillies, sliced
4cm piece of fresh ginger, peeled
    and finely chopped
3cm piece of fresh turmeric,
    peeled and finely chopped

To make the spice paste, use a pestle and mortar to pound the candlenuts and shrimp paste to a fine paste. Add the shallots, garlic, chillies, ginger and turmeric and pound again to a paste.

Rinse the prawns and pat them dry. Trim the lemongrass, bruise the stalk and tie the leaves together in a knot.

Heat the oil in a wok and fry the spice paste for about 3 minutes. Add the lemongrass, salam leaves, lime juice and prawns. Stir-fry for about 3 minutes on a low heat.

Add the coconut milk and tamarind and bring to the boil. Reduce the heat and simmer for about 3 minutes. Season with sugar and salt and serve immediately with white rice.

Sate penyu
turtle satay

Although the sea turtle lives in the unclean sea and shares its home with demons and monsters, it is nonetheless regarded as holy. According to ancient scriptures, the sea turtle played a large part in the earth's formation – in other words, in the creation of Bali. It is said that the island rests on a huge black stone on the back of a giant sea turtle, drifting around in the sea, which is why the Balinese have him to thank for their Earth. Although the turtle is now a protected species and cannot be caught or killed, many locals still regard turtle meat as a delicacy, and it is on occasion consumed, especially after religious ceremonies. With certain ceremonies, there is special dispensation for the event, and one is obliged to make an offering of turtle meat. When preparing this dish, you could use fish or chicken, so that you can at least acquaint yourself with the typical flavours of a turtle dish, if not with the dish in all its authenticity.

makes 12–16/ serves 3–4

500g firm white fish fillet,
  or chicken
50g freshly grated coconut
3 tablespoons grated *gula
  Bali* or palm sugar
50ml thick coconut milk
  (page 184)
juice of 1 leprous lime
  (if unavailable, use a kaffir
  lime)
salt
2 tablespoons coconut oil

flat, wide satay sticks

For the spice paste
½ teaspoon coriander seeds
½ teaspoon white peppercorns
½ teaspoon roasted dried
  shrimp paste
3 shallots, peeled and
  finely sliced
3 garlic cloves, peeled
  and finely chopped
1 long red chilli, deseeded
  and sliced
7 bird's eye chillies, sliced
1 lemongrass stalk,
  finely chopped
1 salam leaf, finely sliced

Cut the fish into small pieces. Toast the coconut in a dry frying pan until golden. Next, pound it in a mortar until the oil is released.

To make the spice paste, use a pestle and mortar to pound the coriander seeds, peppercorns and shrimp paste to a fine paste. Add the shallots, garlic, chillies, lemongrass and salam leaf and pound again to a paste.

Mix the spice paste with the *gula Bali* or palm sugar, toasted coconut, coconut milk, lime juice and salt. Using your hands, knead this mixture into the fish and shape onto satay sticks.

Grill the satays on both sides over a charcoal fire or under a hot grill until brown and cooked through, brushing regularly with the coconut oil. Serve with white rice and *Lawar Kacang* (page 134).

Kenus pelalah

squid with spicy coconut milk sauce

As preparing coconut milk takes time, you may prefer to buy it ready-made – in which case, read the label carefully. Tins of coconut milk and coconut cream look very much alike, but the cream contains much more fat. I would advise against using blocks of creamed coconut, as this contains even more fat than tinned coconut milk and cream, resulting in a dish with a completely different taste and texture. One more piece of advice: pure coconut milk, without preservatives and thickening agents, is always best.

serves 4

500g small squid
juice of 5 leprous limes
   (if unavailable, use kaffir limes)
1 teaspoon finely ground
   white pepper
salt
3 tablespoons vegetable oil
5 kaffir lime leaves
500ml thick coconut milk
   (page 184)
sprig of lemon basil
granulated sugar

For the spice paste
5 candlenuts
2 teaspoons roasted dried
   shrimp paste
5 shallots, peeled and
   finely sliced
3 garlic cloves, peeled and
   finely chopped
5 long red chillies, deseeded
   and sliced
7 bird's eye chillies, sliced
4cm piece of fresh ginger, peeled
   and finely chopped
3cm piece of fresh turmeric,
   peeled and finely chopped
2 teaspoons tamarind pulp

Clean the squid thoroughly and remove the skin, the wings and the internal sac. Slice each tube into rings and cut the tentacles into small pieces. Put the rings and pieces into a bowl with the lime juice, pepper and a little salt, and set aside to marinate for 15 minutes.

To make the spice paste, use a pestle and mortar to pound the candlenuts and shrimp paste to a fine paste. Add the shallots, garlic, chillies, ginger, turmeric and tamarind and pound again to a paste.

Heat the oil in a wok and fry the spice paste for about 3 minutes. Stir in the squid and lime leaves and fry briefly on a high heat. Add the coconut milk, reduce the heat and add the leaves of the lemon basil and sugar to taste. Simmer for about 3 minutes and serve with *Nasi Putih* (page 147).

Vegetables

The Balinese like green on their plate.

Volcanic eruptions on Bali have resulted in a layer of extremely fertile topsoil. Vegetables do not only grow in gardens but also along the roadside. Over the centuries, the Balinese have shown a great creative talent in developing vegetable dishes. It seems as if every plant can inspire them to invent and make a special dish to feature it. There is a saying among foreigners that 'the Balinese like green on their plate', indicating the vital part vegetables play in the daily meal. Of course, the Balinese predilection for vegetables also has an economical background – they are the cheapest foodstuff provided by the island. Vegetables as they appear on the Western table were not originally familiar to the Balinese: cauliflower, carrots, broccoli and cabbage, to name but a few, had never been seen on Bali before the advent of tourism. These days, various popular Western vegetable varieties are now permanent features at the markets and in the kitchen, due entirely to the influence of tourism. The visitors' demand for these vegetables grew by leaps and bounds, and they are now commercially grown in the higher, cooler parts of Bali. In fact, the combination of the climate and fertile soil on Bali proved to be ideal for the cultivation of Western vegetables.

Authentic Balinese vegetable dishes are usually prepared with the young leaves of plants and trees that grow in the vicinity of the houses. Shoots of the bamboo plant are very much in demand, and the same goes for the marrow of the trunk of a young banana tree. Name any plant or tree and in most cases the Balinese will succeed in making a tasty dish out of it. The methods of preparation

vary greatly. Sometimes the Balinese just briefly blanch the vegetables, mix them with grated coconut or some herbs and spices, and serve them in this simple way. Vegetables are also cooked in coconut milk, then briefly stir-fried in a wok with some oil.

The leaves are not the only part of the plant used; in some cases flower buds are transformed into a flavourful dish, in particular the flower bud of the banana tree and that of the ginger plant. Then there are fruits, picked unripe before the sweetness has developed, and prepared and eaten as a vegetable: papaya, mango and jackfruit all straddle both categories. If rice is the main staple of Balinese cuisine, vegetables come a close second. Both are essential components of any meal, and because vegetables are so cheap – and sometimes even free – several vegetable dishes are often served with a meal. Balinese cuisine has a reputation for being spicy, and indeed some indigenous leaf vegetables have a unique aroma and distinct natural spiciness.

One leaf that is not in itself edible but plays a significant role in the kitchen is that of the banana tree. This green leaf serves as a wrapping for any meat, fish and poultry dish that is steamed or grilled. As it heats up, it infuses the food inside the parcel with a distinct flavour. It is this unique flavour that characterises so many Balinese dishes.

stir-fried cassava leaves

This vegetable dish uses the young, tender and soft leaves of the cassava or manioc, which is called the 'potato of the tropical world'. The cassava is easily grown in dry ground and is cheap, especially the leaves of the plant. *Begala* is very popular among Balinese people, who consider this a typical dish from their island. It is also used in the preparation of *Be Guling* (page 34). Balinese cooks sometimes prepare *Be Siap Guling* (page 63) and *Bebek Betutu* (page 77) with *begala* instead of the original stuffing.

serves 4

500g cassava leaves, washed
3 tablespoons coconut oil
5 shallots, peeled and
    finely sliced
3 garlic cloves, peeled and
    finely chopped
3 bird's eye chillies, sliced
3cm piece of fresh lesser
    galangal, peeled
2cm piece of fresh turmeric,
    peeled
3cm piece of fresh galangal,
    peeled
1 lemongrass stalk, very
    finely chopped
salt

Put the cassava leaves into a large pan of boiling water. Cook for about 15 minutes until tender, then drain well.

Heat the oil in a wok and add the shallots, garlic, chillies, lesser galangal, turmeric, galangal and lemongrass and fry for 2 minutes. Add the cassava leaves and stir-fry for a further 3 minutes. Season with salt and serve.

Bergedel jagung

corn fritters

In the distant past, the Spanish brought corn from the New World to the Far East, where it quickly became established. On Bali, ears of corn are often sold as snacks along the roadside, and on large car parks where tourist buses stop for breaks. The freshly picked ears of corn are cooked or roasted in their husks and the soft, sweet kernels eaten straight off the ear.

makes about 20/serves 4–6

4 fresh ears of corn or 100g
  frozen sweetcorn kernels
6 shallots, peeled and
  thinly sliced
3 garlic cloves, peeled
  and thinly sliced
1 long red chilli, deseeded
  and finely sliced
3 bird's eye chillies, sliced
1 teaspoon roasted dried
  shrimp paste
1cm piece of fresh ginger,
  peeled and finely chopped
2cm piece of fresh lesser
  galangal, peeled and
  finely chopped
2cm piece of fresh turmeric,
  peeled and finely chopped
2cm piece of fresh galangal,
  peeled and finely chopped
12 tablespoons vegetable oil
2 eggs
4 tablespoons plain flour
2 tablespoons rice flour
3 kaffir lime leaves, very
  finely chopped
salt

If using fresh corn, hold each ear on its end on a chopping board and scrape off the kernels with a sharp knife.

Use a pestle and mortar to pound half the shallots, the garlic, chillies, shrimp paste, ginger, lesser galangal, turmeric and galangal to a paste.

Heat the oil in a wok and deep-fry the remaining shallots until golden and crisp. Using a slotted spoon, scoop them onto kitchen paper and leave to drain.

Beat the eggs in a bowl and add both flours, the corn kernels, lime leaves, spice paste, deep-fried shallots and enough water to make a thick and fluid batter. Season with salt.

Reheat the oil, add tablespoonsful of batter, three or four at a time, and deep-fry for 3–4 minutes until golden brown. Remove to kitchen paper to drain, then serve.

Gedang mekuah

young papaya in spicy sauce

An example of a fruit cooked as a vegetable. In Balinese cuisine, several fruits such as papaya, mango and jackfruit are prepared in their unripe state as vegetables, and eaten as such. The Balinese find *gedang mekuah* a cheap dish, as papayas grow everywhere and are sold on the markets for next to nothing. The flesh of a ripe papaya is orangey red, whereas the flesh of an unripe fruit is often still white.

serves 8

1kg green (unripe) papaya
1 lemongrass stalk
2 tablespoons vegetable oil
5 salam leaves
3 kaffir lime leaves
500ml water
salt

For the spice paste
1 teaspoon coriander seeds
1 teaspoon roasted dried shrimp paste
2 teaspoons white peppercorns
1 teaspoon black peppercorns
7 shallots, peeled and finely sliced
3 garlic cloves, peeled and finely chopped
3 long red chillies, sliced
5 bird's eye chillies, sliced
2cm piece of fresh lesser galangal,
   peeled and finely chopped
3cm piece of fresh turmeric,
   peeled and finely chopped
6cm piece of fresh galangal,
   peeled and finely chopped
salt

Peel the papaya, cut it in half and scoop out the seeds. Cut the flesh into pieces about 4cm long, 4cm wide and 1cm thick.

Use a pestle and mortar to pound the coriander seeds, shrimp paste and peppercorns to a fine paste. Add the shallots, garlic, chillies, lesser galangal, turmeric, galangal and a little salt and pound again to a paste.

Trim the lemongrass, discarding any tough outer leaves, bruise the stalk and tie the remaining leaves together in a knot.

Heat the oil in a wok and fry the spice paste for about 3 minutes. Stir in the lemongrass, salam leaves, lime leaves, water and papaya. Season with salt, then bring to the boil. Reduce the heat and simmer for 20 minutes until the papaya is tender.

Jukut nangka
stir-fried jackfruit

Coriander seeds, as used in this dish, stimulate the production of stomach juices which are responsible for a quick and proper digestion.

serves 4

500g young jackfruit
salt
1 lemongrass stalk
3 tablespoons vegetable oil
300ml thick coconut milk
   (page 184)
2 salam leaves

For the spice paste
1 teaspoon coriander seeds
1 teaspoon roasted dried
   shrimp paste
½ teaspoon white peppercorns
½ teaspoon black peppercorns
7 shallots, peeled and
   finely sliced
5 garlic cloves, peeled
   and finely chopped
4 long red chillies, deseeded
   and sliced
6 bird's eye chillies, sliced
6cm piece of fresh galangal,
   peeled and finely chopped
6cm piece of fresh turmeric,
   peeled and finely chopped
2cm piece of fresh lesser
   galangal, peeled and
   finely chopped

To make the spice paste, use a pestle and mortar to pound the coriander seeds, shrimp paste and peppercorns to a fine paste. Add the shallots, garlic, chillies, galangal, turmeric and lesser galangal and pound again to a paste.

Wash the jackfruit and cut into pieces of about 3cm. Put the pieces into a pan with plenty of water. Add a little salt, bring to the boil and cook for about 25 minutes. Drain.

Trim the lemongrass, bruise the stalk and tie the leaves together in a knot.

Heat the oil in a wok and fry the spice paste. Add the lemongrass, coconut milk and salam leaves. Season with salt and add the jackfruit. Cook, stirring, for about 45 minutes or until the jackfruit is tender.

Jukut ares

young banana tree stem in spicy chicken broth

On Bali, this dish – made with the marrow of a young trunk of the banana tree – is seldom eaten at home, but must be included when *Be Guling* (page 34) is prepared, which only happens on feast days in or near the temple. However, *jukut ares* is often prepared at the *pasar malam*, the evening markets, where *be guling* is sold. Instead of the marrow of the banana trunk, this dish can also be prepared with the flower buds of the banana tree. The resulting dish is then called *serosop*.

serves 4

500g banana heart from a
 young banana tree stem
salt
1 lemongrass stalk
1 litre water
3 tablespoons *Base Megenep*
 (page 185)
3 salam leaves
½ teaspoon finely ground
 white pepper
½ teaspoon finely ground
 black pepper
500ml chicken stock
12–15 tablespoons vegetable oil
7 shallots, peeled and
 finely sliced

Cut the tender heart of the banana tree stem into very thin slices. Put the slices in a roasting tin, sprinkle with salt and set aside for 1 hour.

Squeeze out as much liquid as possible from the slices, then repeat the process a couple of times until the pieces are dry and soft. Rinse in cold water and drain well.

Trim the lemongrass, bruise the stalk and tie the leaves together in a knot.

In a large pan, bring the water, lemongrass, *base megenep*, salam leaves and the white and black pepper to the boil. Boil until the water has almost evaporated. Add the chicken stock and banana heart slices and simmer for 10 minutes until the banana heart slices are tender but still just firm to the bite.

Heat the oil in a wok and deep-fry the shallots until golden and crisp. Using a slotted spoon, transfer them to kitchen paper and leave to drain.

Serve the banana heart dish with the deep-fried shallots.

Jukut belimbing
star fruit leaves with spicy sauce

The star fruit tree is another of Bali's cure-alls – there is a Balinese saying that star fruit tea three times a day keeps the doctor away. The leaf is used to alleviate itching, by being bruised and then rubbed over the itchy area. To make the tea, the leaves are cut, bruised and boiled, then drained. The tea is believed to help lower high blood pressure.

serves 2–3

300g star fruit leaves
3 tablespoons coconut oil
2 tablespoons *Base Megenep*
  (page 185)
3 salam leaves
200ml thick coconut milk
  (page 184)
1 teaspoon sugar
salt and finely ground
  black pepper

In a large pan of boiling salted water, cook the star fruit leaves for about 7 minutes. Drain well.

Heat the coconut oil in a wok and fry the *base megenep* for about 3 minutes. Add the salam leaves, coconut milk, star fruit leaves and sugar. Season with salt and pepper and simmer for about 5 minutes on a low heat. Serve.

Jukut buah kacang

spicy yard-long beans

I specify here that the yard-long beans should be cut in pieces, but any elderly Balinese hearing that would immediately berate me and say that I should not cut, but break, the yard-long beans. Why? There is no apparent explanation, but on Bali it is said that a dish with yard-long beans is much tastier when the beans have been broken instead of cut. Try it for yourself.

serves 4–6

500g yard-long beans
1 lemongrass stalk
12–15 tablespoons vegetable oil
5 shallots, peeled and
    thinly sliced
150g *Base Megenep* (page 185)
3 salam leaves
150ml thick coconut milk
    (page 184)
salt

Wash the yard-long beans, trim them and cut them into lengths of about 3cm. Trim the lemongrass, bruise the stalk and tie the leaves together in a knot.

Heat the oil in a wok and deep-fry the shallots until golden and crisp. Using a slotted spoon, transfer them to kitchen paper and leave to drain.

Pour all of the oil out of the wok. Add the *base megenep*, lemongrass, salam leaves, coconut milk and a little salt and bring to the boil. Add the yard-long beans and cook for about 5 minutes until the beans are tender but still with a little bit of bite, and the liquid has almost evaporated. Serve with the deep-fried shallots.

chayote with spicy coconut sauce

On its own, the flesh of this pear-shaped fruit has hardly any flavour at all, which is why it needs many different herbs and spices added to it.

serves 4

500g chayote
1 lemongrass stalk
12–15 tablespoons vegetable oil
7 shallots, peeled and
  finely sliced
125ml water
3 salam leaves
½ teaspoon finely ground
  white pepper
½ teaspoon finely ground
  black pepper
2 tablespoons *Base Megenep*
  (page 185)
150ml thick coconut milk
  (page 184)
salt

Peel the chayote, discard the seed and cut the flesh into 2cm cubes. Trim the lemongrass, bruise the stalk and tie the leaves together in a knot.

Heat the oil in a wok and deep-fry the shallots until golden and crisp. Using a slotted spoon, transfer them to kitchen paper and leave to drain.

Put the water, chayote, lemongrass, salam leaves, white and black pepper, and *base megenep* in a pan and bring to the boil. Reduce the heat and simmer for about 15 minutes. When the chayote is tender but still has some bite, add the coconut milk and cook for a further 5 minutes. Season with salt.

Just before serving, sprinkle with the deep-fried shallots.

Jukut paye

stir-fried bitter gourd

The name of this vegetable already says it: the taste is bitter. Rubbing the bitter gourd
slices briefly with salt and rinsing them will remove some of the bitterness.

serves 4–6

2 bitter gourds
3 tablespoons coconut oil
2 shallots, peeled and
   thinly sliced
2 garlic cloves, peeled and
   thinly sliced
1 long red chilli, deseeded
   and sliced
3 bird's eye chillies, sliced
1 teaspoon dried shrimp paste
½ teaspoon sugar
salt

Halve the gourds lengthways, scrape out the seeds and cut both
halves into thin slices.

Heat the oil in a wok and fry the shallots and garlic for 2 minutes.
Add the chillies and shrimp paste and stir-fry for 1 minute.

Add the sliced gourd and sugar. Season with salt and stir-fry for
about 5 minutes. Serve.

Jukut keliklik

braised yard-long bean leaves
in spicy sauce

This is another almost forgotten Balinese dish which I fear may be relegated to oblivion in the near future. In the past, the leaf of yard-long beans was only eaten by the poor, and many people now use the leaves from the harvest of yard-long beans as cattle feed. Outside of Asia, these leaves will be very hard to find, but you could use green bean leaves instead.

serves 4

3 bunches of yard-long
　bean leaves
100g fresh coconut
2 teaspoons tamarind pulp
3 tablespoons water
3 salam leaves
salt

For the spice paste
3 shallots, peeled and
　finely sliced
3 garlic cloves, peeled and
　finely chopped
4 bird's eye chillies, sliced
3cm piece of fresh ginger, peeled
　and finely chopped
2cm piece of fresh lesser
　galangal, peeled and
　finely chopped
1cm piece of fresh galangal,
　peeled and finely chopped
1 lemongrass stalk,
　finely chopped
3 tablespoons coconut oil

To make the spice paste, use a pestle and mortar to pound the shallots, garlic, chillies, ginger, lesser galangal, galangal and lemongrass to a paste. Stir in the coconut oil.

Wash the bean leaves and cook them in a large pan of boiling water for about 10 minutes, then drain. Remove the dark brown skin from the coconut and grate the flesh finely. Mix the tamarind pulp with the water.

Bring about 200ml of water to the boil in a wok. Add the grated coconut and cook for about 3 minutes.

Add the spice paste, tamarind water, cooked leaves and salam leaves, season with salt and simmer for a further 5 minutes. Serve.

Jukut rambanan

yard-long beans, bean sprouts and jackfruit in thick coconut sauce

On Bali, it is common knowledge that galangal (*laos*) has various medicinal properties; *laos* tea is drunk to heal skin disorders. Galangal tea with a teaspoon of honey dissolved into it alleviates coughing and helps to heal bronchitis.

serves 4–6

300g yard-long beans
250g bean sprouts
250g young jackfruit
1 lemongrass stalk
12–15 tablespoons vegetable oil
4 shallots, peeled and
  thinly sliced
1cm piece of fresh galangal,
  peeled and finely chopped
3 salam leaves
2 tablespoons rice flour
300ml thick coconut milk
  (page 184)
1 teaspoon finely ground
  black pepper

For the spice paste
5 shallots, peeled and finely sliced
3 garlic cloves, peeled and
  finely chopped
3 long red chillies, deseeded
  and sliced
1 teaspoon roasted dried
  shrimp paste
2cm piece of fresh ginger,
  peeled and finely chopped
1cm piece of fresh lesser galangal,
  peeled and finely chopped
2cm piece of fresh turmeric,
  peeled and finely chopped

Trim the yard-long beans and cut them into lengths of about 3cm. Wash the bean sprouts and pinch out the green 'tails'. Blanch the beans in a pan of boiling salted water for about 4 minutes, and the bean sprouts for 3 minutes. Drain and plunge them into cold water, then drain again.

Peel the jackfruit, cut into slices and cook for 20 minutes in plenty of boiling water until tender. Trim the lemongrass, bruise the stalk and tie the leaves together in a knot.

To make the spice paste, use a pestle and mortar to pound the shallots, garlic, chillies, shrimp paste, ginger, lesser galangal and turmeric to a paste.

Heat the oil in a wok and deep-fry the shallots until golden and crisp. Using a slotted spoon, transfer them to kitchen paper and leave to drain.

Pour all but 3 tablespoons of the oil out of the wok, add the spice paste and stir-fry for about 3 minutes until golden. Add the galangal, salam leaves and lemongrass. Mix the rice flour with the coconut milk and add to the wok. Stir constantly until the sauce has thickened. Stir in the pepper.

Arrange the vegetables next to each other on a platter, pour over the sauce and serve garnished with the crisp shallots.

Jukut ulih

bean sprouts and yard-long beans in spicy coconut sauce

Bean sprouts, which come from the soya and mung beans, are a very healthy vegetable, packed with vitamin C.

serves 4–6

250g yard-long beans
150g bean sprouts
12–15 tablespoons vegetable oil
3 shallots, peeled and finely sliced
juice of 1 leprous lime
   (if unavailable, use a kaffir lime)
3 salam leaves
150ml thick coconut milk (page 184)
salt

For the spice paste
3 candlenuts
1 teaspoon roasted dried
   shrimp paste
1 garlic clove, peeled and
   finely chopped
1 long red chilli, deseeded and sliced
7 bird's eye chillies, sliced
2cm piece of fresh lesser galangal,
   peeled and finely chopped

Trim the yard-long beans and cut them into lengths of about 3cm. Wash the bean sprouts and pinch out the green 'tails'. Blanch the beans in boiling salted water for about 4 minutes, and the bean sprouts for 3 minutes. Drain and plunge them into cold water, then drain again.

To make the spice paste, use a pestle and mortar to pound the candlenuts and shrimp paste to a fine paste. Add the garlic, chillies and lesser galangal and pound again to a paste.

Heat the oil in a wok and deep-fry the shallots until golden and crisp. Using a slotted spoon, transfer them to kitchen paper and leave to drain.

Pour all but 3 tablespoons of oil out of the wok, add the spice paste and stir-fry for about 3 minutes. Add the lime juice, salam leaves and coconut milk. Season with salt and simmer for about 5 minutes.

Arrange the vegetables next to each other on a platter, pour over the sauce and serve garnished with the crisp shallots.

Jukut urap
mixed vegetables with coconut

This is another typical ceremony or temple dish, largely unknown outside of Bali and Indonesia. In my Amsterdam restaurant, this crunchy mix of vegetables and coconut was much in demand!

serves 4–6

100g bean sprouts
100g yard-long beans
100g spinach
flesh from 1 fresh coconut
1cm piece of fresh lesser
    galangal, peeled and
    finely chopped
1 teaspoon black peppercorns
salt
2 kaffir lime leaves, very
    finely chopped
150g *Sambal Mbe* (page 156)
1 teaspoon granulated sugar
juice of 2 leprous limes
    (if unavailable, use kaffir
    limes)

Wash the bean sprouts and pinch out the green 'tails'. Trim the yard-long beans and cut them into small pieces. Wash the spinach thoroughly. Blanch each vegetable separately for 3–4 minutes in boiling salted water. Drain, refresh in cold water and drain again.

Remove the dark brown skin from the coconut, toast the flesh over hot coals or under the grill until light brown, then grate it coarsely.

Use a pestle and mortar to pound the lesser galangal with the peppercorns to a fine paste, then season with salt.

Put the blanched vegetables into a serving dish and stir in the lime leaves, *sambal mbe*, sugar, lime juice, salt, coconut and spice paste.

black pigeon beans cooked in coconut milk

Many Balinese dishes have names starting with *jukut*. People have asked me countless times what this word means, and the answer is really quite unexciting: it translates simply as 'vegetables'.

serves 4–6

500g black pigeon beans
3 shallots, peeled and
   finely sliced
2 garlic cloves, peeled and
   thinly sliced
1 teaspoon roasted dried
   shrimp paste
1 long red chilli, deseeded
   and sliced
3 bird's eye chillies, deseeded
   and sliced
2cm piece of fresh lesser
   galangal, peeled and
   finely chopped
500ml thick coconut milk
   (page 184)
1 salam leaf
salt

Soak the pigeon beans overnight in plenty of cold water. Drain and put into a large pan. Cover with cold water, bring to the boil, skim and boil rapidly for 10 minutes. Reduce the heat and simmer for about 1 hour until tender. Drain.

Using a pestle and mortar, pound the shallots, garlic, shrimp paste, chillies and lesser galangal to a paste.

Add the coconut milk, spice paste and salam leaf to the beans. Season with salt and simmer, uncovered, on a gentle heat until the liquid has evaporated. Serve with white rice.

Kacang base kalas

yard-long beans with spicy coconut milk

I adore this dish. Each time I eat it I am transported back to the days of my youth. Close to the hotel in Denpasar where I lived with my mother and father, fresh *kacang base kalas* was prepared at a tiny roadside stall. I often crept out just before bedtime to grab a portion of this wonderful dish, but I was not always lucky enough not to be caught by my parents.

serves 4

300g yard-long beans
2cm piece of fresh lesser
   galangal, peeled and
   finely chopped
2cm piece of fresh turmeric,
   peeled and finely chopped
2cm piece of fresh galangal,
   peeled and finely chopped
1 teaspoon *gula Bali*
   or palm sugar
½ teaspoon ground white pepper
100ml thick coconut milk
   (page 184)
4 tablespoons *Sambal Mbe*
   (page 156)
salt

Wash the yard-long beans and cut each in half. Bring a large pan of salted water to the boil, add the beans and cook for about 3 minutes. Drain and cool.

Use a pestle and mortar to pound the lesser galangal, turmeric, galangal, *gula Bali* or palm sugar and white pepper to a paste.

Put the coconut milk in a pan and stir in the spice paste. Bring the mixture to the boil and cook until reduced by half. Set aside to cool.

Mix the yard-long beans with the *sambal mbe* and reduced coconut milk and knead together until the beans are soft and pliable. Season with salt and serve.

water spinach with *sambal pelecing*

This is truly a dish for those who love nicely spiced piquant food, and I am certainly one of them!

serves 4

500g water spinach
150g *Sambal Pelecing*
  (page 162)

Discard the tough stems from the water spinach and wash the leaves thoroughly. Bring a large pan of water to the boil. Add the spinach and cook for about 15 minutes until tender. Drain well.

Mix the cooked spinach with the *sambal pelecing* and serve.

seaweed salad with spicy coconut

To many people, seaweed is a relatively new, or even still unknown, vegetable. On Bali, seaweed has been an ingredient for centuries, sold in nearly every market and in many different varieties. Since seaweed has become popular outside of Asia as a 'healthy' vegetable, several companies have sprung up on Bali, to cultivate and harvest it. In a relatively short time, seaweed has become an important export.

serves 6

400g fine seaweed, white or green
100g fresh coconut flesh
½ teaspoon roasted shrimp paste
150ml *pindang* water (page 189)
3 bird's eye chillies, sliced
1cm piece of fresh galangal,
  peeled and chopped

Wash the seaweed. Bring a large pan of water to the boil. Add the seaweed and cook for about 5 minutes. Drain and leave to cool.

Toast the coconut flesh over coals or in a hot oven and grate finely. Use a pestle and mortar to pound the shrimp paste and mix in the *pindang* water.

Combine all the ingredients and serve as a snack.

Lawar daun belimbing

star fruit leaf salad

Many herbs and spices are used to prepare home remedies for all manner of afflictions. For example, the leaf of the star fruit is used to combat rheumatism: a handful of leaves is pounded with nine cloves and fifteen black peppercorns, after which a dash of vinegar is added. This mixture is then used to massage the afflicted body parts. Balinese people do not throw away any parts of vegetables or meat. This explains the use of gizzards in this traditional recipe.

serves 4

5 candlenuts
3 black peppercorns
1 quantity *Base Wangenan*
   (page 185)
1 bunch of star fruit leaves
5 chicken hearts
5 chicken gizzards
4 tablespoons coconut oil
3 shallots, peeled and
   finely sliced
3 garlic cloves, peeled and
   finely chopped
3 long red chillies, deseeded
   and sliced
3 bird's eye chillies, sliced
3 tablespoons thick coconut milk
   (page 184)
juice of 1 leprous lime (if
   unavailable, use a kaffir lime)
salt

To make the spice paste, use a pestle and mortar to pound the candlenuts and peppercorns to a fine paste. Add the *base wangenan* and pound again to a paste.

Wash the star fruit leaves. Rinse the chicken hearts and gizzards and cut them into small pieces.

Bring a large pan of water to the boil. Add the star fruit leaves and cook for about 15 minutes, then drain.

Heat about 2 tablespoons of the coconut oil in a wok and fry the shallots, garlic and chillies for about 3 minutes. Transfer the mixture to a plate.

In the same wok, heat the remaining oil and fry the spice paste for about 3 minutes. Add the chicken hearts and gizzards and stir-fry for 7 minutes. Add the star fruit leaves, coconut milk, fried shallot mixture and the lime juice. Season with salt and stir-fry for a further 3 minutes, then serve.

Lawar kacang

yard-long bean salad

Yard-long beans are quite common, but if you can't find them in the supermarket or in an Asian shop, use haricots verts or green beans instead. I prefer haricots verts, because their taste is closer to that of yard-long beans. On Bali, yard-long beans are eaten very often. This vegetable grows in many home gardens on a supported vine, because the beans, up to half a meter long, have to hang down.

serves 4–6

200g minced chicken
1 tablespoon melted *gula Bali*
   or palm sugar
250g yard-long beans
250g fresh coconut flesh
12–15 tablespoons vegetable oil
5 shallots, peeled and
   finely sliced
5 garlic cloves, peeled and
   finely chopped
7 bird's eye chillies, sliced
juice of 2 leprous limes (if
   (unavailable, use kaffir lime)
salt

banana leaves, washed
   and patted dry
bamboo strips or
   toothpicks

For the spice paste

5 candlenuts
1 teaspoon black peppercorns
1 teaspoon roasted dried
   shrimp paste
2 long red chillies, deseeded
   and sliced
1cm piece of fresh lesser
   galangal, peeled and
   finely chopped
3cm piece of fresh turmeric,
   peeled and finely chopped
3cm piece of fresh galangal,
   peeled and finely chopped
1 lemongrass stalk,
   finely chopped

To make the spice paste, use a pestle and mortar to pound the candlenuts, peppercorns and shrimp paste to a fine paste. Add the chillies, lesser galangal, turmeric, galangal and lemongrass and pound again to a paste.

Mix the spice paste with the minced chicken and *gula Bali* or palm sugar. Cut a piece of banana leaf about 20 x 25cm and place the chicken mixture on top. Fold both sides of the leaf over the filling. Fold the open ends over and secure the parcels with bamboo strips or toothpicks. Place in a steamer, ensuring it rests above the water. Steam until cooked through, about 20 minutes.

Trim the yard-long beans, wash them and cut them into lengths of about 1cm. Blanch them for 3 minutes in boiling salted water. Drain, refresh in cold water and drain again.

Remove the dark brown skin from the coconut, toast the flesh over hot coals or under the grill until light brown, then grate it coarsely.

Heat the oil in a wok and deep-fry the shallots and garlic separately until golden and crisp. Using a slotted spoon, transfer them to kitchen paper and leave to drain. Fry the bird's eye chillies in the oil and drain on kitchen paper.

Remove the chicken from the banana leaf and mix it with the beans, grated coconut, fried shallots and garlic, chillies and lime juice. Season with salt and serve.

Lawar paku

fiddlehead salad

In Asia, fern sprouts, or fiddleheads, are transformed in many different ways into tasty vegetable dishes. This is the Balinese variety that I was served regularly at home. I like this dish best when it is made with fresh fern sprouts, but they are rarely available outside of Asia. I use canned when I cannot find fresh, but they are not as crunchy, and this somehow affects the flavour as well.

serves 4–6

500g fiddleheads/fern sprouts
100g boneless, skinless
  chicken breast
100g fresh coconut flesh
1 lemongrass stalk
2 kaffir lime leaves
1 tablespoon coconut oil
2 tablespoons *Base Megenep*
  (page 185)
2 salam leaves
100ml thick coconut milk
  (page 184)
75g *Sambal Mbe* (page 156)
salt

Trim the ends off the fiddleheads and wash the tips. Bring a large pan of water to the boil. Add the trimmed fiddleheads and simmer for about 10 minutes. Drain well.

Chop the chicken finely. Toast the coconut flesh over hot coals or under the grill. Peel off the dark brown skin and finely grate the flesh. Chop half the brown skin very finely and discard the remaining skin.

Bruise the lemongrass and tie the leaves together in a knot. Chop the lime leaves very finely.

Heat the coconut oil in a wok and fry the *base megenep* for 1 minute. Add the chopped chicken, lemongrass and salam leaves and stir-fry for about 2 minutes.

Add the coconut milk, bring to the boil, then simmer gently until the liquid has evaporated. Set aside to cool.

Stir the fiddleheads, grated coconut flesh, chopped brown skin, lime leaves and *sambal mbe* through the chicken mixture, season with salt and serve.

Pepes nangka

young jackfruit steamed in banana leaf

I always use this dish to please vegetarians, and when I serve it to non-vegetarians, they are often surprised to find it does not contain any meat.

serves 4–6

400g young jackfruit
3 kaffir lime leaves, very
    finely chopped
salt
1 tomato, cut into wedges
3 salam leaves
1 sprig of lemon basil

For the spice paste
5 candlenuts
1 teaspoon ground coriander
1 teaspoon roasted dried
    shrimp paste
5 shallots, peeled and
    finely sliced
3 garlic cloves, peeled and
    finely chopped
5 long red chillies, deseeded
    and sliced
5 bird's eye chillies, sliced
3cm piece of fresh ginger, peeled
    and finely chopped
3cm piece of fresh turmeric,
    peeled and finely chopped
1 lemongrass stalk,
    finely chopped
2 teaspoons tamarind pulp
salt

banana leaves, washed and
    patted dry
bamboo strips or toothpicks

To make the spice paste, use a pestle and mortar to pound the candlenuts, coriander and shrimp paste to a fine paste. Add the shallots, garlic, chillies, ginger, turmeric, lemongrass, tamarind and a little salt and pound again to a paste.

Wash the jackfruit and cut into cubes of about 3cm. Put the cubes into a saucepan of salted water, bring to the boil and cook for about 25 minutes. Drain well.

In a salad bowl, mix the jackfruit with the spice paste, lime leaves and a little salt. Stir in the tomato wedges and leave to marinate for 2 hours.

Cut a square of banana leaf, about 30cm, and place the salam leaves on top. Put the jackfruit mixture on top and finish with the lemon basil. Fold both sides of the leaf over the filling. Fold the open ends over and secure the parcel with bamboo strips or toothpicks.

Put the parcel in a steamer, ensuring it rests above the water. Cover and steam until cooked through, about 20 minutes.

Rujak kuah pindang

green mango with *pindang* sauce

A dish for real aficionados of Balinese food. Even though the locals love it, from my experience I know that Westerners do not always appreciate it. This is mainly due to the use of *trasi bakar* and the *pindang* water, both of which are known for their pronounced aroma.

serves 4–6

2 green (unripe) mangoes

For the *pindang* sauce
3 bird's eye chillies, sliced
½ teaspoon roasted shrimp paste
150ml *pindang* water (page 189)
salt

Peel the mangoes and, using a serrated knife, cut them into thin slices.

Use a pestle and mortar to pound the chillies and shrimp paste to a fine paste. Add the *pindang* water and a little salt.

Stir the mango slices into the sauce and serve.

vegetables mixed with two sauces

This fairly complicated vegetable dish hails from the area around Gianyar, a town in the centre of Bali, where the many small restaurants and roadside *warung* serve it. But that is not the only reason Gianyar is worth a visit. In the town and surrounding countryside, there are many fine wood carvers and excellent silversmiths.

serves 4–6

about 750g mixed vegetables, such
   as yard-long beans, water spinach,
   bean sprouts, spinach, winged
   beans/asparagus peas

For the peanut sauce
75g roasted peanuts
3 long red chillies, deseeded
   and finely sliced
2 teaspoons dried shrimp paste
juice of 1 leprous lime
   (if unavailable, use a kaffir lime)
100ml water
100ml coconut oil
salt

For the coconut sauce
1 garlic clove, peeled and
   finely chopped
2cm piece of fresh galangal,
   peeled and finely chopped
2cm piece of fresh lesser galangal,
   peeled and finely chopped
2 long red chillies, deseeded
   and finely sliced
3 bird's eye chillies, sliced
1 teaspoon dried shrimp paste
1 teaspoon sugar
salt
150g freshly grated coconut

Wash the vegetables. Cut the yard-long beans into pieces and the water spinach and winged beans into small pieces. Pinch out the 'tails' of bean sprouts. Blanch each vegetable separately in boiling salted water, for 2–4 minutes. Drain.

To make the peanut sauce, use a pestle and mortar to pound the peanuts, chillies and shrimp paste to a fine paste. Add the lime juice, water, coconut oil and a little salt and mix well.

To make the coconut sauce, use a pestle and mortar to pound the garlic, galangal, lesser galangal, chillies, shrimp paste, sugar and a little salt to a paste. Mix in the grated coconut.

Just before serving, mix the vegetables and sauces together.

Tipat cantok

blanched vegetables and pressed rice with spicy peanut sauce

Those who love Indonesian food are undoubtedly familiar with the vegetable dishes *gado gado* and *pecil*. *Tipat cantok* is the Balinese version of these two and has a comparable taste. It is best appreciated when the vegetables are still nicely crunchy, so be careful not to overboil them!

serves 4–6

200g yard-long beans
100g bean sprouts
100g water spinach
1 packet Pressed Rice (page 151)
12–15 tablespoons vegetable oil
11 shallots, peeled and
    finely sliced
1 tablespoon *kecap manis*
prawn crackers or melinjo
    nut crackers

For the peanut sauce
200g roasted peanuts
2 teaspoons shrimp paste
1 teaspoon salted yellow beans
1 teaspoon roasted dried
    shrimp paste
5 bird's eye chillies, sliced
3 garlic cloves, peeled and
    finely chopped
2 tablespoons melted *gula Bali*
    or palm sugar
juice of 3 leprous limes
    (if unavailable, use kaffir limes)
salt

Trim the yard-long beans and cut them into pieces. Wash the bean sprouts and pinch out the green 'tails'. Wash the water spinach. Bring a large pan of water to the boil, add the pressed rice (still in the packet) and cook until firm. Remove the packet from the water and leave to cool.

Bring a large pan of salted water to the boil and blanch the vegetables separately: the yard-long beans for about 4 minutes and the bean sprouts and spinach each for about 3 minutes. Drain and refresh in cold water, then drain again.

Heat the oil in a wok and deep-fry the shallots until golden and crisp. Using a slotted spoon, transfer them to kitchen paper and leave to drain.

To make the peanut sauce, use a pestle and mortar to pound the peanuts, shrimp sauce, salted yellow beans and shrimp paste to a fine paste. Add the chillies and garlic and pound again to a paste. Stir in the *gula Bali* or palm sugar, lime juice, a little salt and enough water to make a thick sauce.

Remove the cooked pressed rice from the packet and cut into cubes. Mix the sauce with the vegetables and the cubed rice. Just before serving, sprinkle with *kecap manis* and garnish with the deep-fried shallots. Serve the prawn crackers separately.

braised banana blossoms

Just as all vegetables are best when fresh, so are the buds of the banana flower, which form the basis of this dish. Flower buds are increasingly available internationally, so there is a chance you will be able to buy them fresh. If you cannot find fresh, they are certainly available canned in many Asian shops.

serves 4–6

1 banana blossom
200g young jackfruit
5 shallots, peeled and
  finely sliced
3 garlic cloves, peeled and
  finely chopped
2 teaspoons dried shrimp paste
5 bird's eye chillies, sliced
3cm piece of fresh lesser
  galangal, peeled and
  finely chopped
12–15 tablespoons vegetable oil
500ml thick coconut milk
  (page 184)
salt

Remove and discard the outer petals of the banana blossom. Peel the jackfruit. Halve the banana blossom and jackfruit lengthways. Bring a large pan of water to the boil. Add the banana blossom and jackfruit and simmer for about 25 minutes until tender. Drain and chop coarsely.

Use a pestle and mortar to pound just over half the shallots, garlic, shrimp paste, chillies and lesser galangal to a paste.

Heat the oil in a wok and deep-fry the remaining shallots until golden and crisp. Using a slotted spoon, remove to kitchen paper and leave to drain.

Pour all but 3 tablespoons of the oil out of the wok. Reheat the remaining oil and fry the spice paste for 1 minute. Add the coconut milk, blossom and jackfruit and season with salt. Simmer for 10 minutes.

Just before serving, sprinkle the dish with the crisp shallots.

Urab base kela

spicy vegetable salad

The *tabia bun*, or long pepper, used in this vegetable dish seems to have disappeared outside of Asia. It was the first variety the Western world came into contact with in the seventeenth century. When the Spanish and Portuguese took it to Europe, the *tabia bun* changed hands for large sums of money. The Europeans attributed exaggerated medicinal properties to this pepper, but its fortunes faded in favour of black and white peppercorns, which the Dutch started transporting in shiploads to the West.

serves 4–6

150g bean sprouts
150g yard-long beans
100g spinach
250g fresh coconut flesh
1 tablespoon coconut oil
2 kaffir lime leaves, very
  finely chopped
150g *Sambal Mbe* (page 156)
salt

For the *base kela*
2 long peppers
1 teaspoon black peppercorns
3 garlic cloves, peeled and
  finely chopped
2cm piece of fresh sweet flag,
  or calamus, peeled and
  finely chopped
2cm piece of lesser galangal,
  peeled and finely chopped

Wash the bean sprouts and pinch out the 'tails'. Trim the yard-long beans and cut them into short lengths. Wash the spinach. Bring a large pan of salted water to the boil and blanch the vegetables separately, each for 3–4 minutes. Drain and refresh briefly in cold water, then drain again.

Peel off the dark brown skin from the coconut and toast the flesh over hot coals or in a hot oven until light brown. Grate the coconut coarsely and chop half the dark brown skin very finely. Discard the remaining skin.

To make the *base kela*, use a pestle and mortar to pound the long peppers, peppercorns, garlic, sweet flag, lesser galangal and the chopped coconut skin to a paste.

Heat the oil in a wok and fry the *base kela* for 1 minute. Stir in the blanched vegetables, kaffir lime leaves, *sambal mbe* and the grated coconut. Season with salt and serve.

Rice

There is no green more exquisite in the world than the green of Bali. The island's breathtaking beauty is largely due to its emerald green rice paddies. From as early as the eleventh century, the Balinese have adopted an ingenious irrigation system for transporting water down from the mountains to flood the *sawas*, the terraced rice paddies. These endless stepped rice fields stretch along the slopes of mountains and hills, and it is often said that they form a stairway to heaven. The paddies start off their growing season bright green, then change over the course of the following five months to silver-grey then burnished gold. Even though they are man-made, they have for centuries been perfectly at one with nature, and are carefully tended by hand.

To this day, rice is still considered a divine food. According to tradition, the goddess Dewi Sri saw to it that this heavenly food became available to humankind. Before the arrival of the rice plant, the Balinese had to make do with the sweet juice of sugar cane and some tubers dug from the soil. Dewi Sri brought rice, which up till then had only been enjoyed by the gods in heaven. Since then, she has been revered as the goddess of rice and agriculture. The Balinese still believe that they depend on the benevolence of Dewi Sri for a plentiful rice harvest. If she is not sufficiently honoured during the growing season, there is every chance she will become angry, resulting in natural disasters followed by a poor or even completely failed harvest. The respect felt for Dewi Sri is evident from the countless shrines and small temples found in the rice paddies, in which offerings regularly take place. A religious ceremony with offerings precedes the rice planting, and during the five months of growth that follow until the harvest, many more rituals

are observed. When the rice grains are large and ripe enough to harvest, the stalks are cut individually with a special knife and bound together in large bundles. The harvest, particularly when it is plentiful, is accompanied by all manner of ceremonies and festivals intended to thank Dewi Sri. This ritual is the start of the numerous sowing, planting and harvest rites that follow. It is often said that the Hindu faith determines the rhythm of life on Bali, but it is not an exaggeration to say that the rice culture has an enormous influence on social life as well. Fearing the loss of a harvest, no Balinese rice farmer will ever forget to perform the necessary rituals and ceremonies.

Rice is always seen by the Balinese as more than mere food; it is also nourishment for the soul. Gratitude for this 'gift of the gods' is evident from the fact that virtually no offering is made that does not include rice. A Balinese has not truly eaten if rice has not formed part of the meal.

Nasi goreng, or fried rice, is one of the most familiar breakfast dishes on Bali, but it is also eaten at other times of the day. *Nasi goreng* basically consists of rice and other dishes left over from the day before. Warmed leftover rice is nothing special, but cooled rice is ideally suited for frying with leftover bits from the day before, because the grains will not stick together. There is no exact recipe for *nasi goreng*; the composition depends mainly on whatever kind of other ingredients are to hand in the kitchen that day.

Nasi jagung
rice with corn

Nasi jagung was born out of poverty and necessity. When rice was still an expensive food, other ingredients, such as corn, were added to bulk it out. This is also the case in other dishes, such as *Nasi Ubi* (page 147).

serves 4–6

500g rice
1 teaspoon salt
150g sweetcorn kernels (fresh or frozen)

Rinse the rice in a colander under cold running water until the water runs clear. Put the rice in a pan and add the salt together with enough water to cover by about 2cm.

Bring to the boil, stir the rice well and cook uncovered for about 5 minutes. Reduce the heat and stir until the water has evaporated.

Stir the corn through the rice. Transfer the mixture to a steamer, ensuring it rests above the water. Cover and steam for about 15 minutes until it is cooked through.

Tip
On Bali, the local rice is used for cooking. For a similar dry, fluffy result, use a mixture of Thai jasmine rice and long-grain rice.

white rice

On Bali, rice is steamed, not boiled. There are many advantages to this method: flavour and aroma stay in the rice and the grains do not break but remain whole. Steamed rice is also more fluffy and less dry than when it is boiled. Another added advantage is that you cannot burn steamed rice.

serves 4–6

500g white rice
750ml tepid water
1 teaspoon salt

Rinse the rice in a colander under cold running water until the water runs clear. Put the rice in a pan and add the warm water. The rice should be covered by about 2cm. Add the salt.

Bring to the boil, stir the rice well and cook uncovered for about 5 minutes. Reduce the heat and stir until the water has evaporated.

Transfer the half-cooked rice to a steamer, ensuring it rests above the water. Cover and steam until tender, about 30 minutes.

rice with cassava

Cassava is also used to make a kind of *krupuk*, similar to prawn crackers. The Balinese enjoy sliced, cooked cassava mixed with grated coconut and a little palm sugar as a sweet snack.

serves 4–6

500g white rice
150g cassava, peeled and cut into
   1cm cubes
1 teaspoon salt

Rinse the rice in a colander under cold running water until the water runs clear. Put the rice in a pan and add the cassava, salt and enough water to cover by about 2cm.

Bring to the boil, stir the rice well and cook uncovered for about 5 minutes. Reduce the heat and stir until the water has evaporated.

Transfer the rice to a steamer, ensuring it rests above the water. Cover and steam until tender, about 15 minutes. Serve the rice with *Sambal Matah* (page 155).

Nasi kuning

yellow rice

Nasi kuning is also called 'festive rice', because it is served at every festive meal for holidays and religious festivals, such as the wedding festival, Hari Raya Kuningan, and anniversaries of temples called Odalan. On Bali, people say that eating *nasi kuning*, or yellow rice, brings luck. Be very careful when using turmeric; it is virtually impossible to remove its stain from clothes. If your hands are stained with turmeric, wash them with lime juice.

serves 4–6

500g white rice
1 lemongrass stalk
1cm piece of fresh turmeric, peeled and grated
125ml thick coconut milk (page 184)
3 salam leaves
1 teaspoon salt

Rinse the rice in a colander under cold running water until the water runs clear. Trim the lemongrass, bruise the stalk and tie the leaves together in a knot. Put the grated turmeric in a sieve above a bowl and press to release the juices.

Put the rice in a pan, add the coconut milk and enough warm water to cover by 2cm. Add the lemongrass, turmeric juice, salam leaves and salt. Bring to the boil and cook uncovered for about 8 minutes.

Stir the rice with a wooden spoon, reduce the heat to a simmer and cook until the water has evaporated. Transfer the half-cooked rice to a steamer, ensuring it rests above the water. Cover and steam until tender, about 15 minutes.

Tip
Nasi kuning can be garnished with strips of omelette, finely chopped chillies, a few celery leaves and chopped cucumber.

Nasi sela

rice with sweet potatoes

To a Balinese, rice is so important that it is served at absolutely every meal.
If, for any reason, it is replaced with something else, within no time he or
she will complain of hunger.

serves 4–6

500g white rice
1 teaspoon salt
150g sweet potato, peeled
   and cut into 1cm cubes

Rinse the rice in a colander under cold running water until the
water runs clear. Put the rice in a pan and add the salt together
with enough water to cover by about 2cm.

Bring to the boil, stir the rice well and cook uncovered for about
5 minutes. Reduce the heat and stir until the water has evaporated.

Stir the sweet potato through the rice. Transfer the mixture to a
steamer, ensuring it rests above the water. Cover and steam for
about 15 minutes until tender. Serve the rice with *Sambal Matah*
(page 155).

Tipat

pressed rice

In each *warung*, or small food stall, you will see small palm leaf
parcels of steamed rice hanging from the ceiling. On Bali, this
is called *tipat* or *ketipat*. Neat little baskets are woven from
palm leaves, and rice is put inside them. The baskets are then
closed and immersed in water until the rice has absorbed the
water and the grains have expanded. Because of lack of space,
the grains of rice are pressed against each other, resulting in a
block of pressed rice. This is a practical and convenient way of
taking a packed lunch to the fields. *Tipat* is served at virtually
every ceremony, not just because it is an easy way of eating
rice, but because the parcels make decorative offerings. Rice
prepared this way also absorbs the flavour and aroma of the
palm leaves.

Sambals

Because rice is the most important dish to the Balinese, and one which they eat several times a day, dishes that are considered main dishes in the West (meat, vegetables, chicken) are often considered side dishes. Yet, some side dishes are indispensable. They are so important that a meal would not be complete if they were not included. Sambals belong in that category. To the Balinese, sambal is a determining factor in any meal. Most sambals have the appearance of a paste-like sauce that is added to dishes during their preparation. Sambals can also be served as condiments to a meal, and these are the lesser-known and drier sambals, of which there are several varieties in Balinese cuisine.

A sambal is piquant, or *pedis* as the Balinese and Indonesians say. The large number of chillies produces a highly seasoned, sharp sauce, which prickles the taste buds so intensely that many Westerners get a shock when they first eat one. Because of a sambal's appealing colour and texture, many Westerners make the common mistake of helping themselves to too much of it. This results in a fiercely stinging and burning reaction in the mouth. Sambals are an acquired taste, but once the fresh and piquant nature of sambals are familiar, they soon become essential components of a meal. Some people even seem to develop an addiction to sambals, distinguishing nuances created by the variety and quantity of chillies used in the preparation.

The best-known chillies are the *lombok* (fresh and long) and *rawit* (bird's eye). The *lombok* is not as hot as the *rawit*. Chillies that are unripe and green are hotter than ripe, red ones. *Rawit* chillies are usually incorporated into a dish in their entirety, whereas *lombok* chillies are usually deseeded, and sometimes the membranes are removed as well.

The capsaicin, the active compound which causes the burning reaction, is mainly stored in the membranes of the chilli and removing them makes the resulting dish less hot.

The so-called dry sambals on Bali have a spicy flavour that is so special that they are sometimes eaten with just steamed white rice. When these sambals are served, other main or side dishes are no longer really necessary. These sambals include *sambal matah* (with shallots, garlic and bird's eye chillies), *sambal mbe* (deep-fried shallots, garlic and bird's eye chillies), and *sambal nyuh* (freshly grated coconut and a typical Balinese herb paste).

As in the rest of Indonesia, prawn crackers and nut crackers appear as side dishes on Bali. These wonderful crisps are served as an accompaniment to a meal and not as a snack, as in the West. *Krupuk* is made from prawns; *emping* is made from the nut of the melinjo tree. *Emping* has a spicy flavour and is often called 'vegetarian *krupuk*.' Besides *krupuk* and *emping*, the Balinese make crisps from cassava and rice flour. These are often eaten as a simple snack.

Sambal bonkot

wild ginger flower *sambal*

The Balinese consumption and use of so many different *sambal* is quite understandable; they have long had a predilection for spicy food, and a meal is not complete without *sambal*. This one is based on the flower of wild ginger, or *bongkot*. Outside of Bali, it is hardly known, which is a pity because it is something really special.

makes about 200g

75g wild ginger flowers
5 shallots, peeled and
   thinly sliced
1 teaspoon roasted dried
   shrimp paste
juice of ½ lime
3 tablespoons coconut oil
30g long red chillies, deseeded
   and shredded
15g bird's eye chillies, sliced
salt

Slice the ginger flowers into narrow strips. Knead them with a little salt and rinse under cold running water. Do the same with the shallots.

Crumble the shrimp paste finely and mix thoroughly with the lime juice and oil. Add the ginger flowers, shallots and chillies, and season with salt.

Sambal matah

fresh sambal

I love the taste of this raw *sambal*, which is prepared all over Bali and is fortunately also served in most tourist restaurants. Many people may have to get used to the flavour and heat, but will quickly become addicted.

makes about 200g

180g shallots, peeled and
   finely sliced
15g garlic cloves, peeled
   and thinly sliced
15g bird's eye chillies, sliced
1 lemongrass stalk, very
   finely chopped
½ teaspoon roasted dried
   shrimp paste
½ teaspoon finely ground
   black pepper
1 teaspoon salt
5 tablespoons coconut oil
juice of 1 leprous lime (if
   unavailable, use a kaffir lime)

Mix the shallots with the garlic, chillies, lemongrass, shrimp paste, pepper and salt. Stir in the coconut oil and lime juice.

Sambal mbe
deep-fried sambal

This is a typical Balinese *sambal* and is a recipe my mother gave to me. It combines beautifully with an array of other Balinese dishes. I experience a unique taste sensation each time I eat this *sambal*, with only a helping of white rice.

makes about 200g

⅛ teaspoon roasted dried
   shrimp paste
salt
12–15 tablespoons coconut oil
150g shallots, peeled and
   finely sliced
25g garlic cloves, peeled
   and finely chopped
8g bird's eye chillies, sliced
juice of 2 leprous limes (if
   unavailable, use kaffir limes)

Use a pestle and mortar to pound the shrimp paste and a little salt to a paste.

Heat the coconut oil in a wok and deep-fry the shallots and garlic separately until golden and crisp. Using a slotted spoon, transfer them to kitchen paper and leave to drain.

Pour all but 2 tablespoons of the oil out of the wok, add the chillies and stir-fry for about 2 minutes.

Remove the wok from the heat and stir in the shallots, garlic, shrimp paste mixture and lime juice.

Sambal megoreng
fried sambal

Getting used to the heat of *sambal* is just a matter of building up resistance. This is why I advise starting with a milder *sambal*, removing the seeds and membranes of the chillies before adding the chillies. If you then rinse the chillies thoroughly under cold running water, they will lose a lot of their heat. Putting cleaned chillies into hot water for five minutes also dampens their fire a bit, but can also take away some of the flavour.

makes about 300g

5 tablespoons vegetable oil
140g shallots, peeled and
  finely sliced
30g garlic cloves, peeled
  and finely chopped
30g long red chillies, sliced
15g bird's eye chillies, sliced

2 teaspoons roasted dried
  shrimp paste
100g tomato, cut into wedges
  and deseeded
5 candlenuts
1 teaspoon granulated sugar
salt

Heat the oil in a wok and fry the shallots, garlic, chillies, shrimp paste and tomato until soft.

Use a pestle and mortar to pound the candlenuts, sugar and a little salt to a fine paste. Add the rest of the ingredients and pound to a paste.

Sambal nyuh
coconut sambal

Sambal nyuh is a very special, exotic side dish, mainly because coconut flesh is the main ingredient. You will almost never find it on the menu in tourist restaurants; this is a dish you see in the food stalls in evening markets, catering mainly to locals rather than tourists.

makes about 200g

125g fresh coconut flesh
75g *Base Gede* (page 185)
1 teaspoon *gula Bali*
  or palm sugar
juice of 2 leprous limes (if
  unavailable, use kaffir limes)
salt

Remove the dark brown skin from the coconut flesh and grate the flesh as coarsely as possible.

Mix the *base gede* with the coconut and add the *gula Bali* or palm sugar, lime juice and a little salt.

Sambal tomat

tomato sambal

One of the mildest chilli pastes in Balinese cooking. It is a refreshing side dish and its mildness can be further accentuated by reducing the number of bird's eye chillies in its preparation. Mind you, a Balinese would shake his head at the thought!

makes about 250g

5 tablespoons coconut oil
60g shallots, peeled and finely sliced
50g long red chillies, deseeded
  and sliced
10g bird's eye chillies, sliced
100g small tomatoes, cut into wedges
1 teaspoon *gula Bali* or palm sugar
½ teaspoon salt

Heat the coconut oil in a wok and fry the shallots, chillies and tomatoes for about 5 minutes.

Leave to cool slightly, then use a pestle and mortar to pound them to a fine paste. Stir in the *gula Bali* or palm sugar and salt.

Sambal sere tabia

sambal with bird's eye chillies and shrimp paste

This is a *sambal* for connoisseurs only. It is an extremely fiery *sambal* made exclusively of bird's eye chillies – by far the hottest chilli pepper in the Balinese kitchen. Even the locals break out into a sweat when they eat this one!

makes about 50g

3 tablespoons coconut oil
2 teaspoons roasted dried shrimp paste
30g bird's eye chillies, sliced
salt

Heat the coconut oil in a wok and fry the shrimp paste and chillies for 2 minutes. Season with salt.

Sambal pelalah

spicy sambal

Always use fresh chillies wherever possible. I know that there are lots of dried peppers, deseeded or not, available, and these have to be soaked before they can be used. They are really only for emergency use, as they lend an unpleasant, sharp taste to the dish they are used in. Fresh chillies are the tastiest.

makes about 200g

1 teaspoon roasted dried
  shrimp paste
4 candlenuts
3 tablespoons coconut oil
40g garlic cloves, peeled and
  finely chopped
40g long red chillies,
  deseeded and shredded

8g bird's eye chillies, cut
  into fine strips
15g fresh ginger, peeled
  and finely chopped
salt

Use a pestle and mortar to pound the shrimp paste and candlenuts to a fine paste.

Heat the coconut oil in a wok and fry the candlenut paste, garlic, chillies and ginger for 3 minutes. Season with salt.

Sambal rajang

chopped sambal

Before *sambal* became an integral part of Indonesian cuisine for their taste alone, they were used to mask the flavour of dishes that were close to spoiling, and to prevent people from becoming ill from them. This was due to the preserving characteristic of chillies – adding them to meat dishes means they take longer to spoil.

makes about 250g

1 teaspoon roasted dried
  shrimp paste
salt
3 tablespoons coconut oil
120g shallots, peeled and
  finely sliced
15g garlic cloves, peeled
  and finely chopped
15g long red chillies,
  deseeded and finely sliced

10g bird's eye chillies, sliced
15g fresh ginger, peeled and
  finely chopped
10g fresh lesser galangal, peeled
  and finely chopped
60g fresh galangal, peeled and
  finely chopped
1 salam leaf, cut into thin strips

Use a pestle and mortar to pound the shrimp paste and a little salt to a paste.

Heat the oil in a wok and add the shrimp paste along with all the remaining ingredients. Fry for 5 minutes.

Sambal tuwung

aubergine *sambal*

Many varieties of aubergine grow on Bali, and nearly all of them can be used for this *sambal*. The white variety is called *tuwung gede*, and the purple variety *tuwung pelung*. Aubergines are used in many different ways, and some varieties are even sliced, sprinkled with some salt and eaten raw. The Balinese consider this a delicacy.

makes about 300g

100g white aubergines
  or 1 large purple aubergine
30g garlic cloves
20g long red chillies, deseeded
5g bird's eye chillies
1 tablespoon vegetable oil
125g tomatoes, peeled and
  quartered
1 teaspoon roasted dried
  shrimp paste

2 kaffir lime leaves, very finely
  chopped
juice of 1 leprous lime (if
  unavailable, use a kaffir lime)
2 tablespoons *kecap manis*
salt

satay sticks

Halve the white aubergines (or cut the purple aubergine into chunks).

Thread the aubergine, garlic and chillies onto satay sticks and sprinkle with the oil. Grill over hot coals or under a hot grill until the aubergine is tender.

Slide the grilled ingredients off the sticks and, when cool enough to handle, peel the aubergine, garlic and chillies. Use a pestle and mortar to pound the grilled ingredients, the tomatoes and the shrimp paste to a coarse paste. Stir in the lime leaves, lime juice and *kecap manis*, then season with salt.

Sambal pelecing

fried *sambal* with lime juice

Garlic is called *bawang putih*, which translates literally as 'white onion'. *Putih* (white) is there to distinguish it from the shallot, which is called *bawang merah* or *bawang barak*, literally translated as 'red onion'.

makes about 250g

60g shallots, peeled
10g garlic cloves, peeled
50g long red chillies,
  de-stemmed
10g bird's eye chillies,
  de-stemmed
1 beefsteak tomato

1 teaspoon roasted dried
  shrimp paste
½ teaspoon salt
½ teaspoon granulated sugar
2 tablespoons vegetable oil
juice of 2 leprous limes
  (if unavailable, use kaffir limes)

Blanch the shallots, garlic and chillies for 1 minute in boiling salted water. Drain. Chop them with the tomato into small pieces and transfer everything to a mortar. Add the shrimp paste, salt and sugar and pound to a fine paste.

Heat the oil in a wok and fry the *sambal*.

Just before serving, sprinkle the lime juice over the *sambal*.

Saur

Balinese *serundeng*

This is the Balinese version of a sweet side dish, that some people may know as part of an Indonesian rice table, often served in the many restaurants on Bali visited by tourists. *Saur* can easily be prepared in larger amounts, because it keeps very well in a sealed container.

makes about 200g

1 tablespoon vegetable oil
30g shallots, peeled and thinly sliced
15g garlic cloves, peeled and
  thinly sliced
30g fresh galangal, peeled and
  finely chopped
4 salam leaves, finely chopped
½ teaspoon ground coriander
1 teaspoon roasted dried shrimp paste
125g freshly grated coconut
¾ teaspoon ground turmeric
¾ tablespoon granulated sugar
¾ teaspoon salt

Heat the oil in a wok and fry the shallots and garlic for about 3 minutes. Add the galangal, salam leaves, coriander and shrimp paste and fry briefly.

Stir in the grated coconut, turmeric, sugar and salt. Stir-fry for about 5 minutes until the coconut is golden brown.

Spoon the *saur* out of the wok and leave to cool.

Sweet delicacies & drinks

The Balinese tend to eat three times a day, but in between there are lots of sweet and savoury snacks. The fact that food is important to the people of Bali is clear from any given street scene, crowded by hawkers of food, simple food stalls, carts and a multitude of small restaurants. You can find something to eat well up to midnight, and often later at one of the many stalls. The food prepared early in the morning at home is often consumed in private. A communal meal around a table is not the Balinese way and only happens when visiting a restaurant. And eating only becomes a social occasion when it occurs after a ceremony in a temple; then people eat together and take plenty of time to enjoy the meal. A meal served in courses, such as we know it in the West, is completely unknown. Soup and main dishes are put on the table simultaneously and eaten with rice.

Desserts do not exist, though it is customary to finish a meal with some fruit. The type of fruit eaten depends on what nature has to offer at that particular time. Thanks to the tropical climate, Bali enjoys a wealth of delicious fruits all year round: pineapples, mangoes, bananas, melons, rambutans, mangosteens, snake fruit, lychees, guavas, star fruit, jackfruit, to name but a few.

One particularly special fruit is the durian. The locals love it, but many tourists are turned off by its penetrating scent. Unfortunately, this prevents many tourists from daring to taste the soft and creamy flesh. But when they do, they discover to their surprise that the scent and taste are two entirely different things. The scent is such that airline companies do not allow the fruit into the passenger cabins.

In tourist restaurants, all kinds of sweets usually eaten as snacks by the inhabitants are served as desserts. The most popular dessert with tourists is *bubuh injin*, a pudding of black rice that the Balinese usually eat for breakfast. Sweet snacks consist mainly of cookies and cakes made with rice or rice flour, banana, coconut and *gula Bali* (palm sugar). These are steamed (in palm or banana leaves), fried or deep-fried. Long ago, and often today as well, these cookies and cakes played an important part in the offerings made to the gods, demons and ancestors on festival days in the temple. *Jaja*, rice flour cookies in all shapes, sizes and colours, were mostly used to decorate the offerings that were piled high and then carried on the head by women to the temple. There are still cookies used exclusively for this purpose and which can only be eaten after the religious ceremony. These are prepared according to an age-old and very simple recipe, and must comply with equally old rules and prescriptions governing their appearance. Most of the time, these rice cookies are depictions of gods and holy animals. Over the course of time, the cookies have become a common sweet snack prepared in the home each morning. Because they have a limited storage life, they are usually sold out by late afternoon at most food stalls.

Batun bedil

rice dumplings in palm sugar sauce

People tell me quite regularly that they think Balinese dumplings are on the rubbery side. When you take a bite, the dumpling will always spring up against the palate. The texture of these dumplings is a result of the cooking or steaming of rice flour. The texture is different when the dough is baked or deep-fried, and these kinds of dumplings are available on every *pasar* (market).

serves 4

100g rice flour
100g tapioca flour
salt

For the palm sugar sauce
300ml thick coconut milk
  (page 184)
50g grated *gula Bali*
  or palm sugar
2 pandan leaves
salt

Mix the rice flour with the tapioca flour, a pinch of salt and enough water to make a dough stiff enough to form balls. Shape into approximately 16 balls of about 2cm diameter.

To make the sauce, put the coconut milk, *gula Bali* or palm sugar, pandan leaves and a pinch of salt in a medium-sized pan and bring to the boil.

Meanwhile, bring a separate pan of water to the boil and add the dumplings. Cook for about 7–8 minutes until tender. Using a slotted spoon, remove the dumplings from the water and drain on kitchen paper.

Add the dumplings to the coconut sauce and simmer for 10 minutes on a low heat. Leave to cool before serving.

Cerorot

rice flour and palm sugar in young coconut leaves

Cerorot is one of the best-known sweet snacks prepared fresh on the market and eaten immediately. If palm leaves for the cones are not available, banana leaves are a good substitute.

makes 20–25

500g rice flour
500g melted *gula Bali*
  or palm sugar
½ teaspoon salt

young coconut leaves,
  washed and patted dry

Put the rice flour in a bowl and slowly add the cooled and melted *gula Bali* or palm sugar, stirring until you have a smooth batter. Stir in the salt.

Make cones with the coconut leaves (see photographs below) and fill them three-quarters full with the batter.

Arrange the cones in a single layer in a bamboo steamer set in a pan over a small amount of water. Cover and steam for 20 minutes until cooked (uncover the pan briefly every 5 minutes to prevent condensation collecting on the cones).

Remove the cones from the steamer and serve as a snack or dessert.

rice flour porridge
with coconut milk and palm sugar

This porridge is eaten as an in-between snack, which is why it is available on each *pasar*, or market. It is a very popular sweet snack with its own particular flavour that is mainly the result of combining *gula Bali* with the vanilla-like aroma of the pandan leaf. It is nearly always served after cremations, although without the *gula Bali*.

serves 4–6

250g fresh coconut flesh
750ml water
3 pandan leaves
100g rice flour
100g melted *gula Bali* or
   palm sugar
½ teaspoon salt

Remove the dark brown skin from the coconut flesh and grate the flesh finely. Stir it into the water and squeeze firmly over a sieve set on a bowl. Measure out 500ml of the liquid into a pan and set aside.

Bruise the pandan leaves, stir them into the remaining coconut milk and leave to steep for 45 minutes. Remove the pandan leaves.

Mix the rice flour, *gula Bali* and salt into the 500ml reserved coconut milk. Add the pandan-perfumed coconut milk and, stirring constantly, bring to the boil. Reduce the heat and, still stirring, simmer until the porridge is thick and creamy.

Serve in bowls and pour a little extra coconut milk over the top.

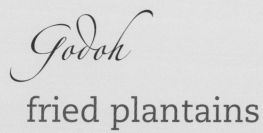

fried plantains

In making *godoh* (better known under the Indonesian name *pisang goreng*), the common banana will not work in place of plantain, as it is far too soft to be deep-fried. The batter is made without eggs, which gives a light, crisp result. On Bali, *godoh* is always eaten with *Unti* (page 180) sprinkled over it.

makes 8–10

175g rice flour
½ teaspoon salt
about 150ml water
2–3 plantains
400ml vegetable oil

Mix the rice flour with the salt and gradually stir in enough water to make a smooth, thick batter. Set aside to rest for 30 minutes.

Peel the plantains, cut them in half lengthways, then cut each piece in half. In a wok, heat the oil. Coat the plantain pieces with the batter and slide them gently into the oil. Deep-fry until golden brown. Using a slotted spoon, remove them to kitchen paper to drain.

black rice pudding

This is the favourite dessert of most of the tourists visiting Bali, and in my restaurant in Amsterdam it was always number one on the dessert menu. I served it with a bit of *santen* (coconut milk) and a scoop of coconut ice cream.

serves 4

100g black glutinous rice
1.5 litres water
5 pandan leaves
100g *gula Bali* or palm sugar
salt
400ml thick coconut milk
(page 184)

Wash the rice in several changes of water and drain. Put into a pan, add the water and pandan leaves and bring to the boil. Cover, reduce the heat and simmer for about 45 minutes, stirring often.

Melt the *gula Bali* or palm sugar in 50ml of hot water, then stir it into the rice. Continue to simmer until thickened. Season with salt. Remove the pan from the heat and leave to cool.

Serve the *bubuh injin* at room temperature. Just before serving, pour the coconut milk over.

coloured rice dumplings with grated coconut and *gula Bali*

When I eat these 'little worms', I always think of my youth. We were very fond of these brightly coloured cakes made of rice flour. Originally, they formed part of temple ceremonies in which this sweet was always offered to the gods first and handed out to the children later. The problem with eating *giling* is that as soon as the 'worms' become moist in the mouth, they stick to the teeth and palate, making conversation virtually impossible!

serves 8–10

300g rice flour
¼ teaspoon limestone powder
150ml tepid water
salt
1 tablespoon pandan extract
1 tablespoon red food colouring
1 tablespoon yellow food
  colouring
250g freshly grated coconut
100ml melted *gula Bali* or
  palm sugar

Mix the rice flour with the limestone powder, water and a little salt and knead to a smooth dough.

Divide the dough into three portions. Mix each portion with a different food colouring (pandan extract is the green one), and shape into little fingers about 5–7mm in diameter.

Bring a large pan of water to the boil and add the dumplings, in separate colour batches. Cook until they float to the surface, which means they are done. Using a slotted spoon, move them to a plate.

Roll the dumplings in the grated coconut, and just before serving, sprinkle them with the *gula Bali* or palm sugar.

Jajas

These are rice flour cookies in all shapes, sizes and colours. They are made from a dough of rice flour and water. This is kneaded by hand and then steamed or deep-fried. I estimate that on Bali, there are about two hundred different shapes and colours in various sizes. *Jaja* are used to this day in temple ceremonies.

Because of their different colours and shapes, they can be turned into the most beautiful offerings. There are ceremonies prescribing how a *jaja* should look, what colour it must be, or in which combination of colours it should be offered. This differs from village to village.

There are ceremonies in which artfully shaped *jaja* towers of more than three metres high are carried by women to the temple on top of their heads. Upon arrival at the temple, the *jaja* tower has to be carefully lowered to the ground and manoeuvred through the temple doors with much turning and sliding – the very brittle cookies cannot be offered once they are broken. After the ceremony is finished, everybody makes a run for the *jaja*, because they are supposed to have special powers after being offered.

Jaja uli
rice cake

The simple list of ingredients indicates that *jaja uli* is a centuries-old snack. This rice cake is prepared with the two most ubiquitous natural ingredients on Bali: rice and coconut. Through the ages, the recipe has remained unchanged and I must admit that I do like the idea of eating a dish that my ancestors had also enjoyed.

500g white sticky rice
125g freshly grated coconut flesh
300g rice flour
1 teaspoon salt

Soak the rice for at least 1 hour in plenty of cold water. Drain thoroughly. Put the rice into a steamer, cover and steam until tender, about 20 minutes.

Transfer the rice to a clean pan and stir in 1.5 litres boiling water. Cover and leave until all the liquid has been absorbed, then set aside to cool.

Mix the coconut, rice flour and salt into the cooled rice and knead to a smooth dough. Put the dough into a steamer, cover and steam until tender, about 20 minutes.

Transfer to a deep mortar (*tumbukan*) and pound it to a firm mass. Shape this into a flat, round cake and leave to cool. Slice the *jaja uli* and smear on some *Tape Ketan* (page 180).

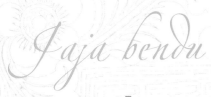

pancakes with hibiscus water

It takes some skill to prepare these almost transparent pancakes. Hibiscus leaves give the batter an aroma that combines beautifully with *gula Bali*, and cannot be likened to any other flavour.

makes about 20

3 hibiscus leaves
150g rice flour

For the *unti*
100g *gula Bali* or palm sugar
50ml water
75g freshly grated coconut
1 pandan leaf

Put the hibiscus leaves with 600ml of water in a pan. Squeeze and knead the leaves, then drain, reserving the water.

Put the rice flour in a bowl and stir in enough hibiscus water to make a smooth batter.

Heat a small, non-stick frying pan. Pour 1 tablespoon of the batter in and swirl it to cover the bottom of the pan. Cook until the top is almost dry and some tiny holes appear. Flip it over and cook for a further 1 minute. Remove to a plate and repeat with the remaining batter.

To make the *unti* filling, in a small pan dissolve the *gula Bali* or palm sugar in the water. Stir in the grated coconut and add the pandan leaf. Heat gently for 5 minutes on a low heat until the liquid has evaporated. Set aside to cool and discard the pandan leaf.

Stack two pancakes on top of each other, spoon a teaspoon of the filling on top and roll up.

Jaja bantal
rice in a pillow

A traditional sweet snack which is always eaten after the ceremony in honour of Odalan, celebrating the birthday of the temple. The young coconut leaves lend the rice mixture a unique aroma. Outside of Asia, it will not be easy to procure young coconut leaves. At a pinch, they can be substituted for banana leaves, but only to the detriment of the authentic flavour of these little rice pillows.

makes about 30

500g white sticky rice
25g raw peanuts
200g freshly grated coconut
1 banana, sliced
¾ tablespoon sugar
salt

young coconut leaves, washed
   and patted dry

Soak the rice overnight in plenty of cold water. Drain thoroughly. In a large pan, bring 750ml of water to the boil. Add the drained rice, cover and bring to the boil. Reduce the heat and simmer for about 30 minutes until tender.

Meanwhile, soak the peanuts for 1 hour in cold water. Drain and chop them finely.

Combine the chopped peanuts, grated coconut, sliced banana and sugar with the rice. Season with salt.

Make pillows (*bantal*) with the coconut leaves (see photograph) and fill them with the rice mixture.

Bring a large pan of water to the boil. Add the pillows and simmer for about 30 minutes. Remove with a slotted spoon.

Klepon Bali

rice flour dumplings filled with palm sugar

The first taste of *klepon Bali*, a traditional post-wedding ceremony treat, usually causes something of a fright. When you bite into the *klepon*, the palm sugar unexpectedly explodes in the mouth, giving rise to quite comical scenes. *Klepon* tastes best when eaten fresh, and if they are left for even half a day, they become dry and tough. Along the access road to the famous Tanah Lot sea temple, there are usually ten *klepon* sellers or more plying their wares to the stream of tourists.

makes 12

150g rice flour
50g cassava flour
5 drops pandan extract
pinch of salt
100g *gula Bali* or palm sugar
150g freshly grated coconut

Mix the rice flour with the cassava flour, pandan extract, salt and enough water to make a stiff dough. Shape into 12 small balls.

Break the *gula Bali* or palm sugar into 12 small pieces. Using a finger, poke holes in each ball and push in a small piece of sugar. Smooth the hole over to close.

Bring a large pan of salted water to the boil. Drop the dumplings in – they will sink to the bottom and float to the surface when they are done. Using a slotted spoon, remove them to a plate.

Roll the boiled dumplings in the freshly grated coconut and serve.

Jongkong sela
steamed sweet potato and coconut in banana leaf

Sweet potato is also used, sliced very thinly and deep-fried, to make *kripik*, the very popular sweet chips.

makes about 20–24

500g sweet potatoes
60g rice flour
200g freshly grated coconut
100g grated palm sugar

banana leaves, washed and
   patted dry

Wash the sweet potatoes and steam until tender, about 30 minutes. Peel when they are cool enough to handle.

Mash the potatoes until smooth, then mix in the flour and grated coconut.

Cut 20–24 squares of banana leaf, each about 10cm. Place two heaped tablespoons potato mixture on each square and top with a small piece of sugar. Fold the leaves to form triangles and fold the edges to seal.

Place the parcels in a steamer, ensuring they rest above the water. Cover and steam until cooked, about 15 minutes.

Kolek biu

plantain braised in sweet coconut milk

Kolek biu is eaten cold, and people often add ice shavings to the banana (in this case plantain) and coconut milk, then serve it as a wonderfully refreshing dessert.

serves 3–4

2 plantains
400ml thick coconut milk
   (page 184)
100g melted *gula Bali*
   or palm sugar
1 cinnamon stick
1 pandan leaf
½ teaspoon salt

Peel the plantains and cut each into 8 pieces.

Put the coconut milk, *gula Bali* or palm sugar, cinnamon stick, pandan leaf and salt into a pan and bring gently to the boil. Add the plantain pieces, reduce the heat and simmer for about 10 minutes. Leave to cool.

Remove the cinnamon stick and pandan leaf before serving.

Pisang rai

cooked plantain with grated coconut

Instead of freshly grated coconut, you can use dried coconut, which is available ready-made. To give dried coconut more aroma, mix it with a little water and briefly steam the mixture.

makes 20

5 plantains
150g freshly grated coconut
salt

For the batter
75g rice flour
½ teaspoon salt
100–150ml water

To make the batter, mix the rice flour, salt and enough water to give a thin consistency.

Cut each plantain into four pieces and coat each completely with the batter. Bring a large pan of water to the boil, gently drop in the pieces of plantain and cook for about 10 minutes. Using a slotted spoon, remove them from the water and drain on kitchen paper.

Dredge the cooked plantain pieces in a mixture of freshly grated coconut and a little salt before serving.

Laklak

Balinese pancakes with grated coconut and palm sugar

This is one of the best-known Balinese desserts and is prepared on the spot in most tourist restaurants. In the *warung* along the roadside and on the market, *laklak* is prepared first thing in the morning and sold until the stock is finished. *Laklak* which has been kept overnight tastes stale.

serves 3–4

250g rice flour
1 teaspoon salt
1 teaspoon limestone powder
coconut oil
100–150g freshly grated coconut
100ml melted *gula Bali* or palm sugar

earthenware mould for small
   round balls, each 4 x 4cm

In a large bowl, mix the flour with the salt and limestone powder. Stir in enough boiling water to make a porridge-like consistency.

Preheat the mould on a gentle heat. Grease the hollows lightly with coconut oil and fill two-thirds full with the batter. Cook on a gentle heat until the bottom is golden and the top is almost dry. Turn them over and cook the other side until golden.

Serve the *laklak* with grated coconut and sprinkle with melted *gula Bali* or palm sugar.

Sumping
rice flour pudding
with plantain steamed in banana leaf

Sago is the flour made from the marrow of the trunk of the sago palm. It is often thought that the marrow is dried and then ground or pounded to a powder, but this is not the case. Sago is the product that comes from mixing the finely ground marrow with water and squeezing the mixture to extract the juice. The squeezed out 'milk' is left to settle for some time. The resulting sediment is dried, then ground to a flour called sago.

makes about 30

1 plantain
2 pandan leaves
50g sago flour
60g rice flour
225ml thick coconut milk
  (page 184)
50g grated palm sugar
¼ teaspoon salt

banana leaves, washed and
  patted dry

Peel the plantain and cut into small pieces. Cut the pandan leaves into 3cm squares.

Put the sago flour, rice flour, coconut milk, palm sugar and salt into a pan. Bring to the boil, stirring constantly.

Add the plantain and continue to stir until the mixture has thickened.

Lay two pieces of banana leaves, each 10 x 20cm, on top of each other, put a pandan leaf on these and finally about 2 tablespoons of the banana mixture on top. Fold the banana leaves over to form a neat parcel and fold the ends under the parcel.

Place the parcels in a steamer, ensuring they rest above the water. Cover and steam until cooked through, about 20 minutes.

Rujak manis
fruit salad with sweet and spicy palm sugar sauce

When a young woman is constantly craving *rujak manis*, a rumour will start to circulate that she must be pregnant – the tangy flavour of this tropical fruit salad is very popular with pregnant women. *Rujak* is made of slices of half-ripe mango and slices of half-ripe papaya, belimbing and apple, but can also include other firm tropical fruits in season. Not all tourists are impressed by the flavour of this fruit salad, but the Balinese are very fond of it. *Rujak* is freshly prepared and sold at street stalls everywhere.

serves 6

All different kinds of tropical fruit are suitable for *rujak*. On Bali, the chosen fruit usually depends on what is locally available and affordable. Always use firm-fleshed fruit.

For the sauce
3 bird's eye chillies, very
   finely sliced
1 teaspoon roasted dried
   shrimp paste
2 teaspoons tamarind pulp
salt
100g melted *gula Bali* or
   palm sugar

Cut the flesh of the chosen fruit into pieces.

Use a pestle and mortar to pound the chillies, shrimp paste, tamarind and a little salt to a fine paste. Stir in the *gula Bali* or palm sugar.

Combine the sauce and fruit.

pancakes stuffed with grated coconut

As far as the main meal is concerned, the Balinese love green and spicy food on their plate. But they adore sweets as well and that becomes obvious on a visit to a market. The ingredients of the traditional sweet snacks are nearly always coconut, rice or rice flour, and *gula Bali* – these ingredients have always been both available and cheap.

makes about 12/serves 4

2 eggs
100g rice flour
1 tablespoon sugar
salt
300–350ml thick coconut milk
  (page 184)
vegetable oil

For the *unti*
100g *gula Bali* or palm sugar
50ml hot water
75g freshly grated coconut
1 pandan leaf

Beat the eggs lightly in a bowl. Beat in the rice flour, sugar, a pinch of salt and enough coconut milk to make a runny batter.

To make the *unti*, in a small pan dissolve the *gula Bali* or palm sugar in the hot water. Stir in the grated coconut and add the pandan leaf. Heat gently for 5 minutes on a low heat until the liquid has evaporated. Set aside to cool and discard the pandan leaf.

Heat a non-stick frying pan. Wipe the pan briefly with kitchen paper dipped in oil, and add about 2 tablespoons of batter to the pan. Swirl the pan so the batter is spread all over and fry on a medium heat until the top is almost dry and some tiny holes appear. Don't turn the pancake over. Put the *unti* filling on the unfried side and roll the pancake up so the filling is completely encased. Turn out onto a plate and repeat with the remaining mixture until it is used up.

fermented sticky rice

Keep the *tape* in a cool place and serve as a spread.

250g black sticky rice
750g white sticky rice
3g *ragi* (page 189) or fresh yeast

banana leaves, washed and
  patted dry

Wash both kinds of rice separately. In separate bowls or pans, soak the black sticky rice for 24 hours and the white sticky rice for 5 hours, in plenty of cold water.

Drain both kinds of rice, combine and put into a steamer. Cover and steam until tender, about 30 minutes. Set aside to cool.

Mix the cooled, steamed rice with the yeast, wrap in banana leaves and leave to ferment for 5 days in a dark place.

white sticky rice cake with *gula Bali*

Cinnamon was brought to Indonesia from Ceylon (now Sri Lanka) by the Dutch. The variety now grown on Bali is cassia (*kesingar* or *kecingar*), which is not as refined, although very suitable for savoury dishes.

makes about 16 squares

100g white sticky rice
1 pandan leaf
1 cinnamon stick
salt
50g *gula Bali* or palm sugar
75ml thick coconut milk
   (page 184)

Rinse the rice under cold, running water for about 5 minutes, then soak it in 300ml of cold water in a pan for about 3 hours.

Add the pandan leaf, cinnamon and salt to the pan and bring to the boil. Reduce the heat and simmer, stirring continuously, for 30 minutes, until the water has evaporated.

Meanwhile, dissolve the *gula Bali* or palm sugar in 50ml of water over a low heat.

Stir this syrup and the coconut milk into the rice. Put everything into a steamer, cover and steam for about 15 minutes.

Spread the rice mixture in an ovenproof dish, about 20 x 20cm, and press to make a 3cm-thick layer. Smooth the surface and leave at room temperature to cool.

Cut into 16 squares of about 5cm and serve.

Brem

rice wine

Brem is an alcoholic drink comparable in appearance and flavour to Campari. The Balinese love this wine made from red glutinous rice and make it at home. In recent years, *brem* has become a big Balinese export product, and everywhere the tourists go the drink is sold in beautiful bottles and jars. *Brem* also forms the basis of *arak*, a gin-like beverage that is always consumed during cock fights. The priest, whom the Balinese call *pemangku*, starts nearly each ceremony with offering some *brem* and *arak* to the demons.

250g black sticky rice
750g white sticky rice
6g *ragi* (page 189) or fresh yeast

banana leaves, washed and
  patted dry

Wash both kinds of rice separately. In separate bowls or pans, soak the black sticky rice for 24 hours and the white sticky rice for 5 hours, in plenty of cold water.

Drain both kinds of rice, combine and put into a steamer. Cover and steam until tender, about 30 minutes. Leave to cool.

Mix the cooled, steamed rice with half of the *ragi* or yeast, wrap the mixture in banana leaves and leave to ferment for 5 days in a dark place – this is *Tape Ketan* (page 180).

Put the fermented sticky rice in a fine sieve set above a bowl. Squeeze the liquid out of the mixture and discard the rice. Combine the liquid from the rice with the remaining *ragi* or yeast and ferment in a dark place for about another 2 weeks. Strain the liquid.

Daluman

gel leaf jelly with coconut milk

On Bali, people say this jelly is not just delicious but also very healthy, due to its high antioxidant content. This makes about 500ml of jelly and keeps for a few days, all you need to do is top each new glass up with coconut milk and a bit of palm sugar.

300g green gel leaf
500ml water

To serve
thick coconut milk
salt
200ml palm sugar syrup

Wash the green gel leaves. Bruise them with a pestle and squeeze out the liquid. Mix the liquid with the water and set aside for about 3 hours until a jelly-like substance has formed.

Season the coconut milk with a little salt. Put 2 tablespoons of the jelly in a long drinking glass, top with 150ml coconut milk and sprinkle with 2 teaspoons of melted palm sugar.

Tuak
palm beer

Tuak is made from the flowers of the sugar palm tree. Before the flowers open, the top of the bud is cut off and the sap is collected in a bamboo container during the course of an afternoon. The following morning, the container is collected and the sap allowed to ferment naturally, after which it can be drunk.

The sap can also be cooked to create palm sugar at the end of the day, before it has fermented.

basic ingredients

Santen

Santen, or coconut milk, is not the water in the coconut, but a liquid that is prepared using the grated fresh or dried flesh of the coconut. The following recipes require the flesh of a 750g coconut. Instead of freshly grated coconut, use 500g of desiccated or 250g of frozen coconut.

Santen asli
thick coconut milk

makes about 500ml

Grate the flesh of one coconut, mix with 250ml of tepid water and soak for 15 minutes.

Squeeze and knead the soaked coconut in the water. Strain, pressing out all the liquid, through a fine sieve set above another bowl.

Santen cair
thin coconut milk

makes about 500ml

Mix the soaked and squeezed coconut used for the *santen asli* with 500ml of tepid water and soak for 15 minutes.

Squeeze and knead the soaked coconut in the water. Strain, pressing out all the liquid, through a fine sieve set above another bowl.

basic spice mixtures

Most authentic Balinese dishes are characterised by the inclusion, taste and aroma of *base megenep*, *base wangenan* and *base gede*. They are a rich mix of herbs and spices, which are used in the preparation of many vegetable and meat dishes. These spice mixtures are not found in any other cuisine in the world. No one on Bali can explain how they came into being and why people combine certain specific herbs and spices for these mixtures. Over the centuries, the rules for preparing them have been handed down from father to son (because it is mainly men who use them in preparing the food for the temple ceremonies). By now, each Balinese housewife knows the composition of it by heart. She always has the mixtures or the necessary ingredients to hand. These days you can buy them freshly prepared at many markets. The composition can vary slightly, depending on the region or village.

Base megenep
hot spice paste

makes about 600g
1 teaspoon roasted dried shrimp paste
80g shallots, peeled and thinly sliced
40g garlic cloves, peeled and thinly sliced
5 long red chillies, deseeded and sliced
4 bird's eye chillies, sliced
100g fresh ginger, peeled and finely chopped
50g fresh lesser galangal, peeled
  and finely chopped
80g fresh turmeric, peeled and finely chopped
165g fresh galangal, peeled and finely chopped
1 lemongrass stalk, very finely chopped
1 teaspoon salt
50ml coconut oil

Use a pestle and mortar to pound the shrimp paste to a paste.
Add the shallots, garlic, chillies, ginger, lesser galangal, turmeric,
galangal, lemongrass and salt and pound again to a paste.
To prolong the shelf life of the spice paste, heat the coconut oil in
a wok and fry the mixture until golden brown. Leave to cool and
store in the fridge for up to 3 months in an airtight jar.

Tip
For a coarse paste, chop the ingredients finely instead of
pounding them in a mortar.

Base wangenan
spice mixture

makes about 5 tablespoons
5 candlenuts
2 teaspoons ground coriander
1 teaspoon cumin
1 tablespoon finely ground black pepper
1 teaspoon finely ground white pepper
1 tablespoon long pepper
1 teaspoon benzoin resin
3 cloves
½ teaspoon ground nutmeg
1 teaspoon fenugreek
1 teaspoon cassumunar ginger
1 teaspoon sweet flag (calamus)

Use a pestle and mortar to pound all the ingredients to a fine
powder, then wrap in cheesecloth. Store in an airtight jar.

Base gede or Base wayah
spice mix

makes at least 300g
4 kaffir lime leaves
4 salam leaves
2 tablespoons coconut oil
2 teaspoons *Base Wangenan*
300g *Base Megenep*

Finely chop the kaffir lime leaves and salam leaves. Heat the
coconut oil in a wok and fry the leaves and the *base wangenan* for
1 minute. Leave to cool. Mix all the ingredients together and store
in an airtight jar for up to 2 months.

glossary of ingredients

Ares (Bal: *gedebong*/Ind: *pohon pisang*): The heart or core of the banana trunk of the banana tree.

Aubergine (Bal: *tuwung*/Ind: *terong*): Vegetable/fruit of a tropical plant (Lat: *Solanum melongena*), also known as eggplant.

Banana (Bal: *biu*/Ind: *pisang*): The elongated, curved, yellow fruit of the banana tree (Lat: *Musa paradiciaca*), which is very common on Bali. There are many different varieties of banana.

Banana blossom (Bal: *pusuh*/Ind: *jantung pisang*): The blossom of the banana tree, used as a vegetable.

Banana leaf (Bal: *don biu*/Ind: *daun pisang*): The leaf of the banana tree that, among other things, is used as a wrapping to steam or roast food in. In most Asian countries, banana leaves can be bought fresh. In Western countries, they are mostly bought frozen. To prepare, take the leaves out of the freezer and keep them at room temperature for 15 minutes, then hold them for just a few seconds over a flame or fire. Wipe them clean with a wet cloth and polish them with a little oil. To avoid breakage, always use a double layer of leaves.

Bean sprouts (Bal: *utik-utik*, *kecambah*/Ind: *taugé*): Produced by allowing the beans of soya or mung to germinate and sprout. Unlike mung bean sprouts, soya bean sprouts must be briefly cooked before eating.

Benzoin (Bal: *menyan*/Ind: *haju haminjon*): The dried resin that is obtained from the trunk of the benzoin tree (Lat: *Styracacea*). This is found in the tropics and only grows upwards of 200 metres above sea level. The tree is very rare. By tapping into a notch in the bark of the trunk, a yellowish liquid is slowly exuded, which when dried turns brown and hard. The dried resin is later processed into an incense-like product often used in ceremonies for its special odour. On Bali, benzoin is used in small quantities in some dishes to give them a special aroma.

Bird's eye chilli/Rawit (Bal: *tabia kerinyi, tabia cenik*/Ind: *cabe rawit*): A member of the *lombok*/long chilli family (Lat: *Capsicum frutescens*). The bird's eye chilli is smaller and much hotter than the *lombok*. The seeds and membranes are not usually removed before adding to dishes. Bird's eye chillies are used in their green (unripe) form and in their red (ripe) form. The green chilli is hotter than the red.

Bitter gourd (Bal: *paya tanduk*/Ind: *paria*): Bitter gourd (also known as bitter cucumber, bitter melon or balsam pear) is the fruit of the climbing plant (Lat: *Momordica charantia*), from which hanging, warty and bumpy gourds or 'cucumbers' grow. These fruits are yellow on the outside and red inside. The ripe flesh has a sweet flavour. Unripe bitter gourds are eaten as vegetables or hollowed out and stuffed with meat or fish and served as a complete dish.

Calamus (Bal: *Jangu*/Ind: *Jangu*: Calamus (common sweet flag) is often found growing wild. The white rhizome (which when dried turns pink) is used in the Balinese kitchen for its spicy odour and bitter flavour.

Candlenut (Bal: *tingkih*/Ind: *kemiri*): The extremely oily, white nut of the candlenut tree (Lat: *Aleurites moluccana*) resembles a large hazelnut or chickpea. The nuts have a rock-hard shell and require considerable strength to get to the kernel. For this reason, candlenuts are usually sold shelled. Candlenuts must be cooked or roasted before use. Shelled nuts quickly become rancid and must therefore be stored in an airtight container. They can also be successfully stored in the freezer. Macadamia nuts can be used as a substitute, but they are sweeter than the lightly bitter candlenut.

Cardamom (Bal: *kapulaga*/Ind: *kapulaga*): The pod of a ginger-like plant (Lat: *Amomen cardamomum*) that in cooking is usually used in its powdered form. It is the inner black or brown seeds that give the most fragrance to this spice. Sometimes the whole pod is used in a braised dish. The pods are not edible and are taken out of the dish before it is served.

Cassava (Bal: *ubi*/Ind: *ketela pohon*): A shrub (Lat: *Manihot utilissima*) that grows 2–4 metres tall. On Bali, it still grows wild. The leaves can be used as greens (leaf vegetables). The elongated tuber can be cubed or sliced and eaten raw, cooked or deep-fried. It also forms the basis of countless sweet and savoury snacks. See also *Tapioca flour*.

Cassumunar ginger (Bal: *banggele*/Ind: *bengle*/Lat: *Zingiber cassumar*): A spice commonly found on marshy ground. The root is yellow on the inside, has a sharp and bitter flavour and a somewhat unpleasant odour. Cassumunar ginger is often used as a medicinal ingredient. Sometimes known as bangke ginger.

Chayote (Bal: *labu jepang*/Ind: *labu siam*): Light yellow to dark green pear-shaped fruit of 7–20cm long with a smooth or wrinkled skin. The weight varies from 600–900g. The chayote or *labu siam* (Lat: *Sechium edule*) belongs to the pumpkin family and has a mildly sweet flavour. The long, narrow stone is not eaten.

Cincau (Bal: *don daluman*/Ind: *cincau*): Jelly, obtained by kneading the peltate (shield-shaped) leaves of the green gel leaf (Lat: *Cyclea barbata miers*) in water. A green, cloudy pulp forms that then turns into a slippery gelatin.

Cinnamon (Bal: *kayu manis*/Ind: *kayu manis*): The bark of the evergreen cinnamon shrub/tree (Lat: *Cinnamomum zeylanicum*) which is sold in quills or sticks. These are the parchment-thin layers of the inner bark of the young branches. The outer layer also has an aromatic flavour, but is of inferior quality.

Cloves (Bal: *cengkeh*/Ind: *cengkeh*): Cloves are the unopened flower buds of the clove tree (Lat: *Eugenia aromatica*). The buds are reddish purple when picked and turn dark brown during the drying process. Originally the clove tree grew only in the Molucca Islands. The clove has preservative properties and gives dishes an exotic flavour.

Coconut leaves (Bal: *busung*/Ind: *daun kelapa*): The young leaves of the coconut palm, used for wrapping food which is then steamed.

Coconut milk (Bal: *santen*/Ind: *santen*): Coconut milk is made by soaking freshly grated coconut in tepid water. This is later squeezed out through a sieve placed above a bowl. The extracted milky liquid is called *santen* (thick coconut milk or coconut cream) and is an important ingredient in Balinese cuisine. See page 184.

Coconut oil (Bal: *lengis nyuh*/Ind: *minyak kelapa*): The oil that is released and floats to the top when coconut milk is heated. In Balinese cuisine, coconut oil is traditionally used to give dishes an authentic flavour.

Coriander (Bal: *ketumbah*/Ind: *ketumbar*): The seed of the bushy plant (Lat: *Coriandrum sativum*), which has a rather fruity, sweet flavour and combines beautifully with other spices and herbs (for example cumin). Available in its dry form as whole seeds or ground to a powder.

Cumin (Bal: *jinten*/Ind: *jinten*): The seed of the annual plant (Lat: *Cuminum cyminum*), which can grow up to 30cm high. Available in its dry form as whole seeds or ground to a powder.

Fenugreek (Bal: *klabet*/Ind: *klabet*/Lat: *Triogonella foenum-graecum*): Annual plant from the papilionaceous flower family (bean family), with 10cm-long pods containing 10–20 triangular seeds. The seeds are pounded to a powder and used in various dishes.

Fiddleheads/Fern tips
(Bal: *paku, jukut paku*/Ind: *pakis*): The young shoots of the fern (Lat: *Cycas rumphii*) that are used as a vegetable. On Bali, many edible kinds of fern are found.

Galangal (Bal: *isen*/Ind: *laos, lengkuas*/Lat: *Alpinia galangal*): Galangal, known as *laos* in Indonesian, is a member of the ginger family and is similar to ginger in appearance. The rhizomes are used extensively in Balinese cuisine. Galangal has a unique spicy and savoury flavour. See also *lesser galangal*.

Garlic (Bal: *kesuna*/Ind: *bawang putih*/Lat: *Allium sativum*): Powerfully flavoured member of the onion family. An integral component of the typical Balinese flavour.

Ginger (Bal: *jae*/Ind: *jahe*): Perennial Asian plant (Lat.: *Zingiber officinale*). The fleshy rhizomes are an important ingredient in Balinese cuisine. Fresh ginger should be thinly peeled because the most flavoursome part is directly under the skin. Peeled ginger is light yellow and the flesh should feel firm. Dried root ginger should in most instances be bruised first before using.

Gula Bali: See Palm sugar.

Hibiscus leaf (Bal: *don pucuk*/Ind: *daun kembang*): The leaf of the flowering hibiscus (Lat: *Hibiscus rosa-simensis*), a common plant on Bali. A fragrant water is made with the flowers, which is then used in sweet dishes. Outside of Asia, hibiscus is better known as a house plant.

Ikan asin (Bal: *sudang*): Salted and dried cod. It has to be soaked for 24 hours before use and the water refreshed several times.

Ikan teri (Bal: *gerang*): Almost transparent tiny fish no bigger than 12cm, related to Indonesian anchovies. A silver band runs from head to tail along the sides of these glassy fish. They are available dried, frozen, smoked and/or salted.

Jackfruit (Bal: *nangka*/Ind: *nangka*): The jackfruit tree (Lat: *Artocarpus heterophyllus*) from the breadfruit family, grows prolifically on Bali. Because of its outward appearance, this large fruit is sometimes confused with durian, and is used both as a fruit and a vegetable. Jackfruit is obligatory when making up the fruit snack, *rujak*.

Kaffir lime (Bal: *juwuk purut*/Ind: *jeruk perut*): The lemon/lime-like fruit of the tree/shrub (Lat: *Citrus hystrix*). This sour fruit has a thick, bumpy, wrinkled, and most often dull green rind.

Kaffir lime leaf/Citrus leaf
(Bal: *don juwuk*/Ind: *daun jeruk*): The leaf of a lemon-like tree (Lat: *Citrus hystrix*), on which the lemon/lime-like fruit, kaffir lime grows. The leaves are recognisable by the distinctive double sections which give them a figure of eight shape. The leaves give dishes a refreshing lemony flavour. Used in fish dishes, it helps defuse strong smells and flavours.

Kecap: A sauce made from soya beans and indispensable in Balinese cuisine. There are three varieties. *Kecap manis* is sweetened with palm sugar and so is thicker and more syrupy than the other two kinds. This *kecap* is used the most. *Kecap asin*, salty *kecap*, can be used instead of salt in Indonesian cuisine. *Kecap sedang* is a mildly flavoured sweet *kecap*.

Klungah: The still green and extremely tender shell of an immature or young coconut in which the flesh is still fluid.

Lesser galangal (Bal: *cekuh*/Ind: *kencur*): A stemless ground-covering plant (Lat: *Kaempferia galangal*). The strongly subdivided stubby rhizomes are often gnarled and are used in countless Balinese dishes. The rhizome is spicier than greater galangal and has a pronounced aromatic flavour. See also galangal.

Lemon basil/Sweet basil leaf (Bal: *don kecarum*/Ind: *daun kemangi*): The leaf of the sweet basil (Lat: *Ocimum basilicum*) has a strong odour. It is mainly used to flavour fish and meat dishes, but is also used in salads and with vegetables.

Lemongrass (Bal: *see*/Ind: *sereh*): A fragrant herb, closely resembling a sturdy kind of grass – although not a member of the grass family. It is an indigenous plant (Lat: *Cymbopogon citraus*) that multiplies into tall, large clumps, and in Indonesia still grows wild. The white to light green stalks/stems are about the length of a satay stick and are used for their fresh lemon-lime taste. *Sereh* is added to refresh and enrich dishes. Lemongrass stalks should be bruised before use, so that the juices and flavour are readily imparted. Shortly before serving the dish, remove the lemongrass. The tender pale inner leaves can be sliced wafer thin, added to a dish and then eaten.

Leprous lime/jeruk limo (Bal: *juwuk lemo of juwuk kasturi*/Ind: *jeruk limo of jeruk kasturi*): The fruit of a large tree or shrub (Lat: *Citrus amblycarpa*), and related to the lemon. The fruit is small (1½–3cm) and almost round. As it ripens, the colour changes from green to yellow.

Lime (Bal: *juwuk nipis*/Ind: *jeruk nipis*): Related to the lemon. In Balinese cooking, the juice of the lime is often used to add freshness and to complement the other flavours.

Limestone powder (Bal: *kapur sirih*/Ind: *kapur sirih*): Pure white limestone powder.

Lombok (Bal: *tabia of tabia gede*/ Ind: *cabe of lombok setan*/Lat: *Capsicum annuum*): One of the many kinds of chillies and one of the most popular in Balinese cuisine. This long chilli is the most important ingredient in making *sambal*. Most widely known are the green and red varieties. The green *lombok* is the unripe version of the red. If the green *lombok* is not picked, it will ripen slowly in the sun until it becomes red. The green *lombok* is hotter than the red.

Long pepper (Bal: *tabia bun*/Ind: *cabe jawa*): The fruit of a climbing pepper plant (Lat: *Piper longum*) is 1cm long and resembles a black catkin. But the long pepper is actually the result of a few berries fusing to form one large berry. Long pepper is found primarily growing wild on Bali. The flavour is very similar to that of black pepper, although long pepper is slightly milder and sweeter.

Mango (Bal: *poh*/Ind: *mangga*): Tropical tree (Lat: *Mangifera indica*) that grows on Bali. The fruit has green (or greeny yellow/greeny red) skin and is eaten unripe (as a vegetable) or ripe (as a fruit). Slices of mango form an integral part of *rujak*, a popular mix of different fruits combined with shrimp paste, chillies and tamarind.

Pacific bonito (Bal: *bangkluk*/ Ind: *ikan tongkol*/Lat: *Sarda chilensis*): A steely blue fish about half a metre in length (also known as Eastern Pacific Bonito) with mackerel-like stripes along its body. Can be substituted for tuna.

Palm leaf (Bal: *busung*/Ind: *daun kelapa*): The young leaves of the coconut palm that, among other things, are used as a wrapping to steam or roast food.

Palm sugar (Bal: *gula Bali*/Ind: *gula Jawa, gula aren, gula merah*): Sold in slices (where the sugar is allowed to cool in bamboo canes) or in cakes (where the cooling takes place in hollowed-out coconuts). To melt, simply add a small amount of water and hold over a low heat until properly dissolved.

Pandan leaf (Bal: *don pandan*/Ind: *daun pandan*): Also known as the pandanus leaf. Is used to give food a light green colour and also for its vanilla-like flavour. The leaves should be washed and bruised before being used, then removed before serving.

Papaya (Bal: *gedang*/Ind: *gedang*): The fruit of a tree (Lat: *Carica papaya*) that is found everywhere on Bali. The papaya resembles an elongated melon and has juicy orange flesh. The black seeds are not eaten. The leaves of the papaya tree are eaten as a vegetable.

Peanut (Bal: *kacang tanah*/Ind: *kacang tanah*): Produces, among other things, the virtually odourless and tasteless peanut (groundnut) oil. This oil is perfect for preparing Balinese dishes.

Pepper (Bal: *mica*/Ind: *lada*): Both black pepper (*mica selem*) and white pepper (*mica putih*) come from the vine (Lat: *Piper nigrum*) that grows in many Asian countries. After flowering, the plant forms clusters of small round berries, which are green at first before ripening to deep orange/red. Black peppercorns are the whole, but still unripe, fully grown berries. After harvesting, they are dried in the sun and turn black. White peppercorns are the red berries, which after picking are soaked in water. After soaking, the outer red coating is rubbed off. White pepper is milder than black pepper.

Petis udang (Bal: *petis udang*/Ind: *petis udang*): Thick, syrupy paste made from shrimp extract, salt and sugar. This shrimp paste is characteristic of Indonesian cuisine and is essential in making *rujak*.

Pigeon beans (Bal: *undis, kekace*/Ind: *kacang Bali*): Beans of the green shrub (Lat: *Cajanus cajan indicus*) that thrives on dry soil and is found throughout Asia. The ripe beans must first be soaked for a very long time, or even with lengthy cooking they will not become tender enough to be edible. The young pods can be used as vegetables. The beans of this plant can also be off-white, yellow, or brown and black in colour.

Pindang water/Kuah pindang:

Pindang water is brined fish sauce, in which sardines have been soaked for a couple of days. The fish is later removed and the water is used as an ingredient in several Balinese dishes.

Ragi: A mix of flour made from toasted ground rice, garlic and grated galangal. This is then pressed into a block and used in the same way as yeast.

Rice flour (Bal: *tepung baas*/Ind: *tepung beras*): Rice ground to a powder.

Sabah leaf (Bal: *don kayu manis*/Ind: *daun katuk*): The leaf of a bushy plant (Bal: *kayu manis*/Ind: *katuk*/Lat: *Sauropus androgynus*). The Balinese name can cause confusion because it gives the impression the leaf comes from the nutmeg tree, but there is absolutely no relation between the two.

Salam leaf (Bal: *don janggar ulam*/Ind: *daun salam*): The oval leaf of the salam tree (Bal: *janggar ulam*/Ind: *salam*/Lat: *Eugenia polyantha*), which because of its shape is often called Indonesian bay leaf – although the lemony taste of the salam leaf in no way resembles the bay leaf, which has a more bitter taste. Consequently, they are not interchangeable. Salam leaves should

be bruised before being added to various braising dishes, and removed before serving.

Sawa eel (Bal: *lindung*/Ind: *belut*): An eel-like predatory fish, which when mature can grow to more than a metre in length and can weigh up to 500g. It is a freshwater fish and feeds on small crabs, shrimps, worms and small frogs.

Seaweed (Bal: *bulung*/Ind: *rumput laut*): Seaweed is a primitive plant (Lat: *Palmaria palmata*) without leaves, stems or roots. It is a member of the alga family. On Bali, it is a traditional vegetable. There are countless varieties available, each with its own colour and flavour.

Shallot (Bal: *bawang barak*/Ind: *bawang merah*/Lat: *Allium ascalonicum*): A member of the onion family. There are red and yellow varieties and the flavour is more pronounced than that of the ordinary onion. The shallot adds that little extra something, that is essential for an authentic Balinese flavour.

Shrimp paste/Trasi (Bal: *sera*/Ind: *trasi*): An indispensable ingredient in Balinese cuisine. *Trasi* is made by pounding or mashing small shrimps, then mixing them with salt and allowing them to ferment. The resulting product is then pressed into blocks and is ready for use. The fermentation process gives the *trasi* a penetrating and, for many, off-putting odour. This odour largely disappears once the *trasi* is fried or roasted, when the *trasi* becomes *trasi bakar*. *Trasi* has a pronounced flavour, but if a recipe is followed as directed, the strong flavour mellows. You can buy shrimp paste roasted and dried, or you can do it yourself by roastng it over a flame or wrapped in foil in the oven.

Soya bean (Bal: *kacang kejele*/Ind: *kacang kedele*): Soya beans, originally from China, are the seeds of the small furry pods of the soya plant (Lat: *Glycine max*). The beans are rich in protein, vitamins and minerals. The

nutritional value is high and becomes even higher when the beans, in their dried form, are briefly cooked or heated. Soya beans make up the base for countless products used as protein replacements. Two of the best known of these products are tofu and tempeh. Other well-known products include *kecap*, soy sauce, soya milk (can be used as a replacement for cow's milk) and soya oil (a healthy oil for deep-frying).

Star fruit (Bal: *belimbing*/Ind: *belimbing manis*): A refreshing, light green to yellow exotic fruit of the belimbing tree (Lat: *Averrhoa carambola*). The star fruit is aptly named; a cross-section slice looks like a five-pointed star. The riper yellow fruits have a slightly sweeter taste than the lightly acidic taste of greener, unripe fruits.

Sticky rice/Glutinous rice (Bal: *ketan*/Ind: *ketan putih* (white)/Bal: *injin*/Ind: *ketan hitam* (black)): A variety of rice where the grains have not been husked, and so during cooking the grains start to stick together. Cooked sticky rice can be eaten either warm or cold. This kind of rice is mainly used to make rice rolls, which are usually filled with meat, chicken or fish. These are called *lemper* and sometimes contain a sweet filling.

Sweet potato (Bal: *sela*/Ind: *ketela rambat*): These tubers have a mildly sweet flavour and can be boiled, steamed and baked. The young leaves can be used as greens.

Tamarind (Bal: *lunal*/Ind: *asem* or *asam*): The flesh of the long bean pods of the tamarind tree. Because of its acidic flavour and preservative characteristics, it is used in countless dishes.

Tapioca flour (Bal: *kanji*/Ind: *tepung kanji*): Tapioca flour, or cassava, is made by cleaning the roots of the cassava (Lat: *Manihot utillisima*), peeling and grating them, then soaking them in water. After the pulp has been drained, the starch grains are dried and ground. See also *Cassava*.

Tauco (Bal: *taoco*/Ind: *taoco*): A paste made from soya beans and salt.

Tempeh (Bal: *tempe*/Ind: *tempe*): A typically Indonesian version of tofu. In making tempeh, unlike in the preparation of tofu where the soya beans are ground, the beans are fermented whole. During this process, a yeast culture forms which helps break down the indigestible husks on the beans and also helps bind the beans to form blocks or cakes. The resulting cake is firm and has a mild, nutty flavour.

Tofu (Bal: *tahu*/Ind: *tahu*): Soft, spongy product made from ground, pressed and fermented soya beans. Tofu has a neutral flavour and is therefore very versatile and used in countless dishes. It also absorbs flavours from other ingredients very easily. In Indonesia, tofu and tempeh owe much of their popularity to the fact that they are much cheaper than meat.

Turmeric (Bal: *kunyit*/Ind: *kunyit*): A tough rhizome plant (Lat: *Curcuma domestica*) of the ginger family. The dried and powdered rhizome or root is the basis of yellow rice, or *nasi kuning*, which is served at virtually all festive meals.

Water spinach (Bal: *kangkung*/Ind: *kangkung*): A creeping water and swamp plant (Lat: *Ipomua reptans*) and leaf vegetable that is extremely popular on Bali. Only the tender young leaves are eaten. Because of their bitter flavour, the tough stems as well as older leaves are discarded.

Wild ginger flower/Torch ginger (Bal: *bongkot*/Ind: *combrang*): The flower buds of the wild ginger plant (Lat: *Phaeomeria speciosa*), a ginger-like spice, which has forked yellow or red rhizomes. The buds as well as the leaves are eaten raw or cooked and served as vegetables.

Winged bean (Bal: *klongkang*/Ind: *kecipir*): The four-sided serrated pod of the winged bean is found on the tropical climbing plant (Lat: *Psophocarpus tetragonolobus*), which is grown in gardens all over Bali. The pods, young shoots and young leaves are all eaten as vegetables.

Yard-long beans (Bal: *kacang, kacang lentor, kacang lantang, kacang dawa*/Ind: *kacang panjang*/Lat: *Vigna sinensis*): Yard-long beans (sometimes also called asparagus beans) can grow up to a metre long. They are prepared like green beans, and are usually more sturdy and have a more pronounced flavour than green beans. They should be washed in the same way as green beans and cut into required lengths according to the instructions in the recipe.

Yard-long bean leaves/Asparagus bean leaves (Bal: *don kacang lentor, don kacang lantang of don kacang dawa*/Ind: *daun kacang panjang*): The leaves of the plant (Lat: *Vigna sinensis*) on which the yard-long bean grows.

CONVERSION CHART

Weight (solids)

7g	¼oz	425g	15oz	30ml	1fl oz	1 litre	1¾ pints
10g	½oz	450g	1lb	40ml	1 ½fl oz	1.2 litres	2 pints
20g	¾oz	500g	(½kg) 18oz	50ml	2fl oz	1.5 litres	2 ½ pints
25g	1oz	600g	1 ¼lb	60ml	2 ½fl oz	1.8 litres	3 pints
40g	1½oz	700g	1 ½b	75ml	3fl oz	2 litres	3½ pints
50g	2oz	750g	1lb 10oz	100ml	3½fl oz		
60g	2 ½oz	900g	2lb	125ml	4fl oz		
75g	3oz	1kg	2/14lb	150ml	5fl oz (¼pint)	**Length**	
100g	3½oz	1.1kg	2½lb	160ml	5½fl oz		
110g	4oz (¼lb)	1.2kg	2lb 12oz	175ml	6fl oz	5mm	¼ inch
125g	4½oz	1.3kg	3lb	200ml	7fl oz	1cm	½ inch
150g	5½oz	1.5kg	3lb 5oz	225ml	8fl oz	2cm	3/4in
175g	6oz	1.6kg	3½lb	250ml	9fl oz	2.5cm	1 inch
200g	7oz	1.8kg	4lb	300ml	10fl oz (1½ pint)	3cm	1 1/4in
225g	8oz (½lb)	2kg	4lb 8oz	325ml	11fl oz	4cm	1 ½in
250g	9oz	2.25kg	5lb	350ml	12fl oz	5cm	2 inches
275g	10oz	2.5kg	5lb 8oz	370ml	13fl oz	7.5 cm	3 inches
300g	10½oz	3kg	6lb 8oz	400ml	14fl oz	10cm	4 inches
310g	11oz			425ml	15fl oz (¾ pint)	15cm	6 inches
325g	11½oz			450ml	16fl oz	18cm	7 inches
350g	12oz (¾lb)	**Volume (liquids)**		500ml	18fl oz	20cm	8 inches
375g	13oz			550ml	19fl oz	24cm	10 inches
400g	14oz	5ml	1 teaspoon	600ml	20fl oz (1 pint)	28cm	11 inches
		10ml	1 dessertspoon	700ml	1¼pints	30 cm	12 inches
		15ml	1 tablespoon or ½fl oz	850ml	11½ pints		

index

Aubergine sambal, 162

Bali, 10-17
Balinese cuisine, 15-17
Balinese serundeng, 163
Banana blossom, braised, 142
Banana tree
  leaves, use of, 9, 114
  young banana tree stem in spicy
    chicken broth, 120
Bananas
  banana braised in sweet coconut
    milk, 176
  cooked bananas with grated coconut,
    176
  fried bananas, 169
  rice flour pudding with banana
    steamed in banana leaf, 178
Bean sprouts
  bean sprouts and yard-long beans in
    spicy coconut sauce, 127
  yard-long beans and bean sprouts in
    thick coconut sauce, 126
Beans
  beef with coconut and beans, 25
  black pigeon beans cooked in
    coconut milk, 129
  yard-long see Yard-long beans
Beef, 18
  beef in sweet kepac sauce, 24
  beef with Balinese spices, 21
  beef with coconut and beans, 25
  beef with spicy sauce, 32
  cooked and pounded beef, 22
  dry spicy beef, 31
  minced beef satay, 29
  spiced beef with coconut, 26
  stewed beef with jackfruit, 27
  sweet and sour beef, 28
Bitter gourd, stir-fried, 124

Cassava
  rice with cassava, 147
  stir-fried cassava leaves, 116
Chayote with spicy coconut sauce, 123
Chicken, 56
  braised marinated chicken, 59
  chicken in spicy coconut milk, 60
  chicken thighs steamed in banana
    leaf, 69
  chicken with Balinese spices, 58
  chicken with pindang sauce, 72
  clear chicken soup, 70
  grilled chicken with coconut milk
    sauce, 63
  grilled chicken with sambal

pelecing, 67
  grilled chicken with sambal sauce,
    62
  minced chicken satay, 74, 75
  roast chicken, 64
  spicy chicken strips, 68
  spicy minced chicken in banana
    leaf, 76
  spit-roasted chicken, 63
  turtle satay, 112
  young banana tree stem in spicy
    chicken broth, 120
Clove jelly with coconut milk, 182
Coconut
  Balinese pancakes with grated
    coconut and palm sugar, 177
  banana braised in sweet coconut
    milk, 176
  bean sprouts and yard-long beans in
    spicy coconut sauce, 127
  beef with coconut and beans, 25
  black pigeon beans cooked in
    coconut milk, 129
  chayote with spicy coconut sauce,
    123
  chicken in spicy coconut milk, 60
  clove jelly with coconut milk, 182
  coconut sambal, 158
  coloured rice dumplings with grated
    coconut and gula Bali, 170
  cooked bananas with grated coconut,
    176
  fried hard-boiled eggs with spicy
    coconut sauce, 82
  goat in spicy coconut sauce, 20
  grated coconut and whitebait salad,
    99
  grilled chicken with coconut milk
    sauce, 63
  king prawns with spicy coconut
    milk, 107
  minced pork with spicy grated
    coconut and sambal mbe, 44
  mixed vegetables with coconut, 128
  pancakes stuffed with grated
    coconut, 180
  rice flour porridge with coconut
    milk and palm sugar, 168
  salad with young coconut and pork,
    46
  seaweed salad with spicy coconut,
    132
  spiced beef with coconut, 26
  spicy ground fish satay with
    coconut, 100
  spicy prawns with coconut in banana
    leaf, 102
  squid with spicy coconut milk
    sauce, 112
  steamed sweet potato and coconut in
    banana leaf, 175
  thick coconut milk, 184

thin coconut milk, 184
  yard-long beans and bean sprouts in
    thick coconut sauce, 126
  yard-long beans with spicy coconut
    milk. 131

Duck, 56
  duck breast satay, 80
  duck with a hot and sweet sauce, 78
  spicy duck roasted in palm leaves,
    77
  spicy minced duck in banana leaf,
    81

Eggs, 56
  fried hard-boiled eggs with sambal
    megoreng, 82
  fried hard-boiled eggs with spicy
    coconut sauce, 82

Fiddlehead salad, 135
Fish, 84
  deep-fried salted fish, 92
  fish and prawn satay, 104
  fish in spicy sour sauce, 98
  fish with spices in banana leaf, 96
  fried fish with chilli sauce, 86
  grilled fish with fresh sambal, 93
  spicy fish grilled in banana leaf,
    94
  spicy fish in banana leaf, 91
  spicy ground fish satay with
    coconut, 100
  turtle satay, 112
Fruit, 164
  fruit salad with sweet and spicy
    palm sugar sauce, 179

Goat, 18
  goat in spicy coconut sauce, 20

Ingredients, 186-191

Jackfruit
  salad with jackfruit and pork, 47
  stewed beef with jackfruit, 27
  stir-fried jackfruit, 119
  young jackfruit steamed in banana
    leaf, 136

Mango, green, with pindang sauce, 137
Meat, 18

Palm beer, 183
Pancakes
  Balinese pancakes with grated
    coconut and palm sugar, 177
  pancakes stuffed with grated
    coconut, 180
  pancakes with hibiscus water, 172
Papaya, young, in spicy sauce, 118
Pork, 18

braised marinated pork, 37
braised pork in onion sauce, 53
fried pork sausages, 43
minced pork satay, 54
minced pork with spicy grated
  coconut and sambal mbe, 44
pork belly barbecued in banana
  leaves, 42
pork in sweet kepac sauce, 39
pork satay with tamarind, 55
pork steamed in banana leaf, 48
pork with Balinese spices, 36
roasted suckling pig with Balinese
  spices, 34
salad with jackfruit and pork, 47
salad with young coconut and pork,
  46
spicy broth with pork, 41
spicy pig's trotter, 33
steamed spicy minced pork in banana
  leaves, 49
stir-fried and stewed pork, 40
Poultry, 56
Prawns
  deep-fried prawns in batter, 108
  fish and prawn satay, 104
  fried spicy king prawns, 110
  grilled king prawns with fresh
    sambal, 106
  grilled prawns and snails in banana
    leaf, 101
  king prawns with spicy coconut
    milk, 107
  prawns in banana leaf, 103
  spicy prawns with coconut in banana
    leaf, 102

Rice, 144
  black rice pudding, 169
  blanched vegetables and pressed
    rice with spicy peanut sauce,
    140
  fermented stick rice, 180
  nasi goreng, 144
  pressed rice, 151
  rice cake, 171
  rice in a pillow, 173
  rice with cassava, 147
  rice with corn, 146
  rice with sweet potatoes, 151
  servings, 9
  sticky white rice, 182
  white rice, 147
  white sticky rice cake with gula
    Bali, 181
  yellow rice, 148
Rice flour
  coloured rice dumplings with grated
    coconut and gula Bali, 170
  cookies, 171
  rice cake, 171

rice dumplings in palm sugar sauce,
  166
rice flour and palm sugar in young
  coconut leaf, 167
rice flour dumplings filled with
  palm sugar, 174
rice flour porridge with coconut
  milk and palm sugar, 168
rice flour pudding with banana
  steamed in banana leaf, 178

Salad
  fiddlehead salad, 135
  grated coconut and whitebait salad,
    99
  salad of star fruit leaves, 133
  salad with jackfruit and pork, 47
  salad with young coconut and pork,
    46
  seaweed salad with spicy coconut,
    132
  spicy vegetable salad, 143
  yard-long bean salad, 134
Sambals, 152
  aubergine sambal, 162
  Balinese serundeng, 163
  chopped sambal, 160
  coconut sambal, 158
  fresh sambal, 155
  fried hard-boiled eggs with sambal
    megoreng, 82
  fried sambal, 158
  fried sambal with leprous lime
    juice, 162
  fried tuna with fresh sambal, 87
  grilled chicken with sambal
    pelecing, 67
  grilled chicken with sambal sauce,
    62
  grilled fish with fresh sambal, 93
  grilled king prawns with fresh
    sambal, 106
  minced pork with spicy grated
    coconut and sambal mbe, 44
  sambal with bird's eye chillies and
    shrimp paste, 159
  sambal with leprous lime juice, 156
  spicy sambal, 160
  tomato sambal, 159
  wild ginger flower sambal, 154
Sardines, fried salted, 88
Sawa eel
  deep-fried sawa eels, 95
  soup with sawa eel, 88
Seaweed
  seaweed salad with spicy coconut,
    132
  seaweed with pindang sauce, 90
Snails
  grilled prawns and snails in banana
    leaf, 101

snails in spicy broth, 109
Soup
  clear chicken soup, 70
  soup with sawa eel, 88
Spice mixtures, 9, 184, 185
Squid with spicy coconut milk sauce,
  112
Star fruit
  salad of star fruit leaves, 133
  star fruit with spicy sauce, 121
Sweet potatoes
  rice with sweet potatoes, 151
  steamed sweet potato and coconut in
    banana leaf, 175
Sweetcorn
  corn cookies, 117
  rice with corn, 146
Sweets, 164

Tomato sambal, 159
Tuna
  fried tuna with fresh sambal, 87
  spicy fish grilled in banana leaf,
    94
Turtle satay, 112

Vegetables, 114
  blanched vegetables and pressed
    rice with spicy peanut sauce, 140
  mixed vegetables with coconut, 128
  spicy vegetable salad, 143
  vegetables mixed with two sauces,
    138

Water spinach with sambal pelecing,
  132
Whitebait
  grated coconut and whitebait salad,
    99

Yard-long beans
  bean sprouts and yard-long beans in
    spicy coconut sauce, 127
  braised yard-long bean leaves in
    spicy sauce, 125
  spicy yard-long beans, 122
  yard-long bean salad, 134
  yard-long beans and bean sprouts in
    thick coconut sauce, 126
  yard-long beans with spicy coconut
    milk. 131